The Patient in Room Nine Says He's God

The Patient in Room Nine Says He's God

Louis M. Profeta, M.D.

BOOKS

Winchester, UK
Washington, USA

First published by O-Books, 2010
O Books is an imprint of John Hunt Publishing Ltd., The Bothy, Deershot Lodge, Park Lane, Ropley,
Hants, SO24 0BE, UK
office1@o-books.net
www.o-books.com

For distributor details and how to order please visit the 'Ordering' section on our website.

Text copyright Louis M. Profeta 2009

ISBN: 978 1 84694 354 6

A CIP catalogue record for this book is available from the British Library.

Design: Stuart Davies

Printed in the USA by Edwards Brothers Malloy

We operate a distinctive and ethical publishing philosophy in all
areas of its business, from its global network of authors to
production and worldwide distribution.

CONTENTS

Preface

The Search for God in the ER

As I grew older and had kids of my own, I was faced with a myriad of robust questions that percolate through the neurons of most men and women as they reach middle age, pouring out of me in a dark, bottomless cup of self-inquiry, introspection.

"Why am I here?"

"Is this all there is to my life?"

"How much time do I have left?"

"Is there really a God . . . and where can I find him . . . or her for that matter?"

So much of Judaism, and most religions, for that matter, focus on us finding God in our everyday lives: from a small, clear stream, to a full moon, to a child's sweet smile. But like any good thing, such sensations become just more of the same. In a lot of ways, godly creations as such heavenly wonders like the raspberry, the scent of an orchid, and the simple spider web become like the sound of an air conditioner or traffic outside our window: the background noise of life that eventually goes unnoticed.

For someone like me, a pure adrenalin junky who thrives on chaos, controversy, and constant motion fed by caffeine to feel alive, finding God in natural settings proved problematic . . . even impossible. No matter how hard I tried, pausing to ponder nature, the gift of life, and the complexities of the ground under foot, the air conditioners of the natural world quickly faded into the background.

So, I stopped and redirected my search, looking at the world I knew best: the ER. If God is really around us, then certainly I could find God in the world of which I am most familiar. It

1

wasn't until I really took stock of the numerous bizarre incidents and the web of subtle relationships that shaped my private and public life as an ER doctor that I realized that all along, God was there: sometimes as a colleague offering needed advice, in the sad look of a child's eyes, or an addict's trembling hand. More often it was a breath of conscience and reason, a voice telling me to pay attention, or a calming hand on the shoulder or a pat on the back.

It was not until I looked carefully that I realized God is not hidden at all. It just takes time, patience, and a bit of energy to develop the mental focus to find him/her in our daily lives. It's like mushroom hunting: it may take you years to finally find one, but once the visual pattern of what you're looking for becomes imprinted in your brain, you realize they're everywhere.

I found God's hand at work in an accidental meeting that years later saved a child's life, in a missed breakfast that took another's, in the passing of a beloved aunt that taught me forgiveness. I found God in a biker's swastika tattoo, in a coma patient's recovery on Christmas Eve, in the voice that saved an ignored patient's life. I found God at a funeral and in the widower's claim that I gave him "forty-eight hours" with his wife. I even found God on an emergency call to a bowling alley with the frames rolling on. Most of all, I realized that God does not need to be found at all: He is everywhere, right in front of your face; he is the stuff that makes up our stuff and all the other stuff in our universe.

This is a collection of stories about my search for God, and how I found him in one of the most emotionally charged environments imaginable: the Emergency Room. By now, I suspect he's somewhat tired of hearing from me, but as long as the calls are free, and the phone number is public knowledge... Well, I think I'll keep calling and waiting to see if his caller I.D. shows up on my life recorder. I'm sure it will.

Chapter One

"The Patient in Room Nine Says He's God"

These words rolled off the nurse's tongue with an odd familiarity and ease. She might as well just have said, "The patient in Room Nine has a sore throat." She casually handed me the chart, then gave me a look like "I didn't sign up for this." Her mouth flashed a tight, linear smile. I glanced at my watch and knew without looking. It was 3:00 A.M. These patients always came in at 3:00 A.M. And it was always at the height of the December flu season when the halls were decked with the ill, the dying, the beaten, and the depressed. I just wanted a few minutes to breathe, perhaps eat a donut; I deserved at least that bit of respite. I glanced over at the nurses' station; if I didn't hurry, only the sugared jellies would be left. I hated jelly donuts. I scanned the chart and looked up at her.

"Really? Why not the mailman or the gas meter guy?" I asked.

"What do you mean?" she asked, unsure of the point I was trying to make.

"I mean, why is it that every nut case is God, Jesus, Satan, or the king of England? Why do they always have to be some government agent or a super secret spy that communicates with aliens or talks to the president through the TV? Why is it they never come into the ER, look around, and whisper, "Pssst, I'm the meterman? Don't tell anyone," or "I'm the cook at Burger King." What is wrong with reading meters, flipping burgers, or delivering newspapers for that matter . . . or even bagging groceries at the local supermarket?"

"Yeah, just once I wish it was God," she said. I grunted in agreement, grabbed the chart and headed down to Room Nine. For a fleeting moment, though, her remark made me pause.

3

Seven, eight, nine. I stopped outside the thick fireproof door. The warm steel handle felt oddly familiar in my hand, sort of like walking into my house.

There is an interesting Judaic legend that tells of 36 Tzadikim Nistarim or hidden, just men. These men are often described as impoverished, homeless wanderers. Many of them do not even know they have been picked by God to bear the sorrow and the sins of the entire planet. When one dies, he is immediately replaced by another.

As long as there is a replacement, then God will spare the world from destruction. But should one no longer be found worthy of being a hidden, righteous man, then the world will end. I would certainly like to think this tale also translates to righteous women as well, but I am merely repeating the legend.

More important, I truly believe the purpose of such tales is to serve as a reminder that we know not the substance or the soul of the person with whom we come into contact. What a tragic legacy if we should be brought before God, and he sits us down in front of a projector screen to play back the scenes of our lives. Lo and behold! We come into contact with one of the righteous 36. We passed him on the street and thought him a bum, ignoring his outstretched hand. We scoffed at his pain. We ignored his fears. We failed as physicians to comfort when we should have been beacons of hope.

About three years ago, I think I met one of the 36. It was the early hours of the morning and we were very busy. I can't recall her name or where she came from, but for a brief moment, I saw her . . . then I saw her again for real.

Medical centers spend millions upon millions of dollars on children's hospitals and child cancer wings, as they should, though the proportion of hospital resources and commercials featuring sick kids seem excessive. Now, please don't misunderstand me. I completely support child-health initiatives. It's just that, for every sick child I put into the intensive care unit, I will admit fifty adults over the age of sixty. Hospital administrators and charitable trusts understand that ill children sell. Snake a tube through a sick child's nose and throw him in front of a camera with a sports hero and, Bang! The dollars fly with instant cash contributions and television coverage. Let's be realistic. A ninety-year-old unresponsive, septic, demented lady in a diaper with Alzheimer's and bed sores does not make for good TV. They don't even make the cut for the television show ER. When was the last time you saw footage of the Dodgers visiting a nursing home or a geriatric ward? When was the last time the Detroit Pistons were at their local dialysis center passing out jerseys and hats? How often do the New England Patriots visit long-term care or retirement centers?

I have a theory that God judges us not so much on how we care for the children, but how we care for the elderly. The child is easy: He or she immediately garners our sympathies. With a quick glance we feel sorrow, compassion. Our hearts ache and our throats knot up as our eyes fill with tears. This is because we are inherently driven to care for the young, to put them under our wing, to shelter them from pain, despair, and harm. The elderly . . . they require work. When I encountered one of the 36 righteous men, I did not recognize 'her'. She was elderly, ill, and disheveled. She had been sent from a nursing home with a spurious reputation. She smelled of soiled undergarments, and her mouth was cracked and dried. She had a dirty catheter extending from her bladder. Her nails were long and unkempt. The elderly woman's hair was white, greasy, and matted to her head. Flakes of dry skin encrusted her hairline.

I hurried into the room with an assembly line sense of importance. I scanned her nursing home chart. I made note of her past history of dementia, sepsis, congestive heart failure, and chronic urinary tract infections. I flew through my exam, no problem. An old, dry, septic catheter urine infection: Antibiotics, call her doc, and make the room ready for the next patient. That was when I truly saw 'her'.

I was leaving the room and glanced up at her lying in the bed. I saw her again. Only that time, she was a child: a soft, clean, vibrantly innocent child. She was playing on a porch somewhere in the Midwest during the 1920s. A small rag doll danced and flayed as she clutched it in her hand. She laughed with her barefoot brother, who was clad in overalls. He chased her around the yard with a grasshopper on his finger. She screamed with laughter. Her father watched from the porch in a wooden rocker, laughing while Mom gently scolded her brother. That was when I saw her taking a ride for the first time in an automobile. It was a small pickup with wooden panels driven by a young man with wavy curls. He smiled gently at her while she sat staring at the road ahead, her hands folded in her lap, clutching a small beaded purse.

That was when I saw her standing in a small church. She was dressed in white cotton, holding hands with the young man, and saying, "I do." Her mom watched with tearful eyes. Her dad had since passed. Her new husband lifted her across the threshold, holding her tight. He promised to love and care for her forever. Her life was enriched, happy.

That was when I saw her cradling her infant, cooking breakfast, hanging sheets, loving her family, sending her husband off to war, and her child to school.

That was when I saw her welcoming her husband back from battle with a hug that lasted the rest of his life. She buried him on a Saturday under an elm, next to her father. She married off her child and spent her later years volunteering at church functions. In time, she lost her friends and disappeared into the nursing home as her mind and her family slowly faded away.

That was when I saw her as a reflection of God: a righteous, pious spirit trapped, crying for help, crying for comfort and dignity. So I went back and put my hand on her cheek. I told her, "I am here. I will take care of you." Though there was no response, I talked about my kids, the weather, how Reggie Miller lit up the Knicks, and how sorry I was that she had to go through all of this discomfort. I helped the nurse clean her off. We washed and combed her hair, scrubbed and gently massaged her hands, and offered her a brief visit into the past.

That was the day my eyes were opened. I didn't know why, it just happened. It was the day I saw a person, not a patient. I saw a soul, not a sickness.

I took a deep breath, and as the door handle fell and the light from the room escaped into the hall, all I could think was, "If you're God, do I have some stories to tell you."

Chapter Two

Scotty

He was the bravest kid I have ever known. I, on the other hand, was an awkward coward, especially around girls. He walked through our young lives with confidence I could only envy and dream of emulating. His name was Scotty, and he was perhaps one of my best boyhood friends. He was short, kind of dumpy, not athletic, an average student, but he had the heart and presence of a Bengal tiger. He was always pushing the envelope: egging houses, playing ding-dong-ditch, sneaking a beer. He would blow up small items with firecrackers, tell outrageous stories about the kids in the neighborhood, and find mischief in something as innocuous as a piece of cake.

While I was always looking around to see who was watching, he charged onward with reckless abandonment. He was a good, pure-of-heart kid, though. He never picked on anyone or teased anybody. The wretched refuse of grade school and junior high were drawn to him like rats to cheese. His younger brother Clark was attached at the hip and they, in all practicality, were an inseparable tandem, Scotty and Clark. Scotty had a way with the opposite sex. He could walk up to any girl, no matter how gorgeous and beyond reproach, strike up a conversation and ask her out on a date. Not bad for a thirteen-year-old. Of course, he was rejected most of the time, but darned if he didn't show up for the game. Most of the time, rejection just seemed to make him all the more determined. We had a symbiotic relationship; I was the cleaner fish and he was the shark. I would live vicariously through his self-confidence, and in return, I cleaned up his messes (or beat the daylights out of anyone who would dare pick on him). Carl learned that lesson in science class.

Carl was everything that Scotty wasn't. He was a disturbed kid who, back at Eastwood Junior High School, was labeled 'a hood'. In seventh grade Carl had shoulder-length hair; he wore black tank tops, Colorado hiking boots, a leather wrist band, and carried a wallet chained to his belt. A pack of cigarettes adorned his front pocket. He was always in fights and seemed mad at the world. He was small for his age and spent his youth aiming to prove himself. When I look back, I feel sad for Carl. I can now only imagine his home life, and as a physician, I understand him better.

For some reason during science class one day when the teacher was out of the room, he decided to single Scotty out for a lesson. He poked fun at him, cursed him, called him "fat boy", slapped him on the back of the head, and so on. He made a spectacle of Scotty in front of the other kids, and all Scotty could do was sit back and take his ridicule. Scotty was not a fighter, and he was certainly no match for Carl. He just did not have the anger in him. I, on the other hand, did. When I told Carl to leave him alone, he turned his attention to me, which was a big mistake for both of us. I was always looking for a fight myself, a cause of the day, and Carl seemed the perfect target.

I had been looking for a reason to come up against this kid ever since I first laid eyes on him. I was, in essence, a tough guy with a conscience. Everything had to be a battle. Every event in my life was a conflict between right and wrong, good and evil, and I was going to be the one to fix it. Carl was that 'back alley sort, the switchblader' we 'good kids' were supposed to avoid. And hell, from social injustice to cause after cause, I jumped the way some people choose shoes. I would try on a battle and if it didn't fit, I would toss it aside and pick another one. The problem was, I left a lot of discarded shoes and damaged soles in my wake.

I used to tell my parents that I never started a fight, when in actuality I started them all; I just didn't throw the first punch.

While I was not a big, tough kid, I was the seventh grade equivalent of Tanner from the *Bad News Bears*, a runt who had a perpetual chip on the shoulder. I was always on the defensive, the silent assassin angry at the whole world, the one who never backed down from anyone but ran for cover when a pretty girl walked up. This, along with my big mouth, got me beat up frequently. But I was the type of kid who would rather have my ass kicked than walk away. In some ways, I am still like this as an adult, though I pick my battles carefully, understanding the ramifications of fighting winless battles.

So Carl turned his attention toward me, called me a few juvenile names, made fun of my clothes, and looked to make sure the class was laughing with him. Then he put his hand on my shoulder, forcing me to sit down (as I knew he would). He started it . . . he touched me first, I would later tell myself and others. BLAM! I proceeded to break Carl's nose in front of the whole class. He fell on his rear and cried. The teacher escorted him out of the room and me to the principal's office. Scotty thought that was the coolest thing he had ever seen. A few weeks later, Carl beat the daylights out of me on the softball field. Oh well, live and learn.

I used to love hanging out with Scotty. He had the newest toys, the most modern model rockets, and he was always in possession of the neatest novelty items. But what made him truly unique was the optimism in which he approached life. He seemed to enjoy every moment of life. He was connected, he knew everything that was going on with everyone in the school, and if he didn't, he would make up the best stories.

"Hey, Lou, see that kid Jeff over there? He beat up a cop on the bus, no kidding . . ." In actuality, Jeff threw an egg at a car while on the school bus; the car belonged to a security guard, who boarded the bus and made Jeff clean it up. I liked Scotty's version better.

I used to spend the night at Scotty's, where we would spend

hours calling girls and playing street hockey until late into the night. After his folks fell asleep, we would occasionally climb out the window and run around the neighborhood, getting into all sorts of trouble. It was nothing serious, just good old-fashioned adolescent mischief, the kind my kids will never be able to get away with under my helm. We were suburban commandos on late-night raids, princes of our domains, sidewalk soldiers. We had no cares and no boundaries: The world was ours. We were eternal kids. And when the time came for me to remove Scotty from life support, I remembered the child whom I called my friend, and I cried for my loss . . . of all those memories, of innocence never to be recaptured.

Scotty was in seventh or eighth grade when he was diagnosed with insulin-dependent diabetes. He struggled with it his entire life. The sad part was that it kept him from pursuing his dream to become a pilot. He married a wonderful girl and had three beautiful children, who became his life, his reason for living. I didn't have much contact with Scotty after he moved in the ninth grade and attended another high school. I got involved in sports, and then went on to college and medical school, though I kept up with him through his parents and mutual friends. I knew that his life had been difficult. He was hard to employ because he was chronically ill and missed long periods of work. But Scotty never complained. He kept plugging along, working when he could, playing his hand of cards as they came. He spent much of his later adult life in and out of the hospital. His heart and intestines were ravaged by his illness, and in time his body buckled under the force of his diabetic cancer.

My wife and I visited Scotty and his family at his apartment in Plainfield, Indiana. It was small, a few bedrooms, and very crowded for a family of five. I felt sad and uncomfortable. By this time I had become a successful, well-to-do physician and it was obvious that he was struggling. What was remarkable about Scotty, though, is that he was happy for my success but was also happy for himself. He was content with his own life and felt he was blessed, even though his health and finances were poor. It didn't matter because he had his wife and his kids, and he was rich beyond Midas.

I was so comforted that Scotty of now was no different from the child of old, when we were kids. We laughed, joked around, and reflected on our early years. We told stories until late into the evening. He was still far more alive and optimistic about the future than I was. Furthermore, he was proud of me. I could tell that he bragged to all of his other friends and family about Louis Profeta, the doctor, the guy in the paper, the writer, the overachiever, and the dude that busted Carl in the chops in science class. I was, in all senses of the word, his undeserving hero; and he was, in all manners of speaking, mine. He still is. He told me that his brother Clark had not fared well in life. He had become an alcoholic and a drug and cocaine addict. It had become so bad that Scotty would no longer allow him in his home or around his children. Not having Clark around, or being able to help him, made Scotty profoundly sad. Scotty knew, as I did, that Clark had crossed the threshold of saving.

During the next few years, Scotty was in and out of the hospital. He had no insurance, but I was able to get him hooked up with a local physician friend. Scotty loved the attention lavished on him in the hospital. The residents took what he perceived as extra good care of him when he was admitted. They made sure to drop my name, informing him that they would face my wrath if he were in pain, or just simply uncomfortable. This, of course, was all a ruse; I've never yelled at a resident physician in my entire life. They knew Scotty was my friend and did me the favor of making him feel all the more important. Scotty was a king and the hospital became a palace. He loved it when I would come to his room and he could call me by my first name in front of the other nurses and physicians. I loved it too.

A few weeks after his last admission for diabetes, Scotty's

heart stopped for a prolonged period of time. He was brain dead. His wife asked if I would take him off life support. Better it is a friend than a stranger, she told me. So, with his wife, his kids, and his other brothers and sisters by his side, I deflated the breathing tube, removed Scotty from the ventilator, and sat while his heart slowed and he gently passed away. Later, I spoke at his funeral, relating my memories of Scotty. His brother Clark somehow made it. He was a shell of the person I once knew. I tried not to get too involved with him, preferring to remember another person in another time. Scotty's wife sat with me and told me Scott had a premonition of his death a few weeks earlier. His demeanor had changed and he cried a lot. He had decided on the spur of the moment to pick the family up and go to Disney World. She said that they had the time of their life. It was, and will always be, the most special memory of their life together.

That day, I came home from the funeral and told my wife to get packed, that we were flying to Orlando the next day. I found a cheap airfare, a room at the Wilderness Lodge, loaded up my two young sons, and flew to Florida. The amazing thing was that we did not wait in line on a single ride. The weather was perfect, and though the park was quite crowded, it seemed that every time we approached a ride, be it the Haunted Mansion, Space Mountain, or those damn spinning teacups, the crowd seemed to evaporate. I knew it had to be Scotty looking out for us. It got to the point where we would walk up to an attraction, thank Scotty, and walk right inside. I have not returned to Disney World since then. There is no way any vacation there could be any better.

Some years later I went to visit Scotty's grave. My sons went with me. We sat on the grass in front of his stone, and I told them stories of my youth. The next day we went to King's Island, an amusement park near Cincinnati. It was the middle of summer and was quite crowded. Once again, we did not wait in line at any of the major attractions, something I always loathed about those parks. We had an absolute blast. We rented a cabana at the water park, where we were just sitting back, relaxing, when I heard a voice.

"Louis . . . Louis Profeta?" And there they were . . . Scotty's mom, dad, and their newly adopted children. They had rented a cabana that happened to be right next to ours. Then I knew. It all made sense . . . Scotty, his parents, the grave, and the amusement park: It was only natural that he was here, too. The day before I had visited him, that day he was visiting me. I had not seen or spoken to his family in nearly five years, and here they were. Once again, the stars had aligned and God gave us a chance to hang out one more time. We caught up on our lives, and his parents met my children. We laughed and reflected on Scotty. I told his new sisters all about the brother they never knew. Later on, we went on more rides and more attractions without waiting in line; my kids would jokingly thank Scotty prior to getting on each ride. I too would smile, look up at the heavens, and thank him and God for a good day.

Chapter Three

An Olympic Legacy

Can an autograph reclaim a life? Can a simple smile, a handshake, or a hug change our destiny or alter the course of a child's existence? Can a kind gesture give one more sunset to the living or comfort the dying? Think not? Then let me tell you a story!

In 1981, I was a seventeen-year-old gymnast for a local high school men's team. How much potential did I have? Who knows? I certainly did not lack in dedication, work ethic, or love for gymnastics. I could reasonably envision myself competing at the collegiate level and perhaps beyond. I had been following the national and international gymnastics' scene with undaunted fervor. I taped every segment the national media aired. The walls of my bedroom were plastered with cutouts of the national men and women's teams. I had a video library of all the greats and studied their routines in detail. I followed the careers of Bart Conner, Kurt Thomas, Mark Casso, Jim Hartung, Scott Johnson, Mitch Gaylord, Peter Vidmar, Tim Daggett, and Phil Cahoy with the same degree of enthusiasm that many of my friends followed baseball. To this day I can recall many of their routines, each twist and each turn. There was, however, one gymnast with whom I was especially captivated: Ron Galimore.

Anyone who knows the sport will tell you that in 1980, Galimore was perhaps the finest vaulter and floor performer in the world. Ron was one of the first to do a full-twisting layout Tsukahara vault in competition. According to 1996 Olympic coach Peter Kormann, no one has yet to do it as well. The height and power that he would obtain off the horse were phenomenal. It was a classic study in the conversion of momentum. There were times that the vault would literally disappear from the TV screen. His power, grace, and air time were unmatched.

But there was also a mystique about Galimore. His father was a famous running back for the Chicago Bears, whose time was cut short by his death in an auto accident. Ron was only six years old at the time. Ron told me that, while he can remember the frigid temperatures of the games, his own image of his father's gridiron play is more a product of other people's memories than of his own. To this day, fans still remind him about his father's greatness. Football, however, took a backseat to another sport. Ron became enamored with gymnastics, and in time accomplished what no other African-American had achieved in the sport. He became a member of the 1980 Olympic gymnastics team, one of the finest American men's teams ever assembled.

There was little doubt in my mind that Ron would take gold on the vault and perhaps a medal on the floor exercise. But then the Soviet Union invaded Afghanistan: Politics and sports came to a screaming collision in 1980 as President Carter announced a U.S. boycott of the Summer Games. In the blink of an eye, a door closed, a dream faded, and the world changed for him.

About a year and a half later, the professional gymnastics tour was scheduled to come to Indianapolis. During an evening practice, I bravely asked Kelly, an attractive young lady who competed in the same gym, to be my date for the event. She said yes, and my confidence soared. I was one of the best male high school gymnasts in Indiana. I was hitting on all my routines, I had tickets to see my heroes perform in person, and my future was right on track. One hour later, I was fighting for my life from a fall on the trampoline. In the blink of an eye, a door closed, a dream faded, and the world changed for me.

When you are young, nothing bad ever happens for the best. It's just bad. I remember lying paralyzed from the neck down, blood filling my mouth, and breathing being harder than from any gymnastics' move I had ever attempted. I knew in an instant my life would never be the same. I caught Kelly's eye as I was transferred into the ambulance: a look of concern melting into a mask of despair. Soon I was strapped to a bed as metal spikes were drilled into my head. I could hear the bones cracking in my skull as weighted traction was applied to stabilize the shattered bones of my spine. I was never as distraught as I was then. I was never so lost. The only constant in my life, outside of my parents, was gone forever.

Gymnastics was my identity; it was who I was at the time. As the pain of the injury dragged on unabated, I began to reflect more and more on my predicament. Fortunately I soon regained the use of my extremities as the swelling in my spinal cord decreased. However, days of traction became weeks. I came to the stark realization that I was nothing more than a 'C-' student with no real skills outside of gymnastics. Depression blinded me to a possible alterative path to the future. But on the evening of the professional tour, I had a revelation and that night my life started to change, a change that sent me off on another journey of self-discovery and fulfillment.

A teammate of mine, Brian Stith, went to the professional gymnastics' tour that I had hoped to attend with Kelly. Somehow he made his way to the floor and told Galimore of my predicament. He related to Galimore that I was perhaps his biggest fan and that a phone call from him might do me some real good. Galimore phoned me at the hospital! Neither Ron nor I can recall much of the discussion, but tears filled my eyes and a tremendous sense of self-worth took hold. I asked him to get a '10' on the vault that night and he did. His words of encouragement were priceless, but more than what he said, it was the simple fact that a stranger who, as a lost seventeen year old, I held in such high esteem would extend a helping hand to someone he had never met. For the first time in weeks, I was smiling for real, not just pretend smiles for my parents. A door opened, a kind gesture turned the knob, and in the blink of an eye, a dream was born. This former 'C-' high school student was going to become a doctor and reach out to others, as Ron had reached out to me.

At the beginning I found college impossible. I had to learn how to be a student. I really had little in the way of academic skills, other than just being smart. I had no test-taking skills, had never taken notes in my life, and I really had no idea how to study. I cruised by in high school, an afterthought in the back of the class. I didn't care about grades, studying, or the SATS. I did just enough to graduate and to get into college.

To this day, I consider the lack of effort I put forth in high school as my biggest mistake. It has, however, made for good comedy, especially early in my career. I returned to Indianapolis and cared for old high school friends, who would look up at me from their hospital beds and exclaim, "You're a doctor? I thought you were like . . . learning disabled or something!"

"Scary . . . isn't it?" I'd always return. Just once I wanted to turn to a nurse and ask, "We better recheck his vitals again, starting with his blood pressure," but I couldn't.

I finished my first semester of college with a respectable 'B' average. For medical school, however, that was a recipe for disaster. In addition, I had to go back and take preparatory classes in English and math. I soon found myself routing my energies from gymnastics into education. The library became my second home, and in four years I knew every good nook and cranny on campus where one could study in peace. In time, one 'A' became straight 'A's'. In 1986, I was accepted to Indiana University School of Medicine. I was later granted admission to the University of Pittsburgh program in Emergency Medicine, one of the most competitive programs in the world. Along the way I managed to pick up more scholarships, plaques, awards, and appointments than I could have ever imagined. I have since had more wonderful experiences as a doctor, and as it usually happens, success can often blind you from whence you came.

In 1997, a child was brought to the emergency department, a very special child. In the blink of an eye, another door was on the verge of closing, another dream was about to fade. And if I had stumbled with my routine, a small life would have been lost forever. The ER was absolute pandemonium that evening and I was exhausted. We had admitted car accident victims, drunks, assaults, heart attacks: It was nonstop, controlled chaos. A young couple brought in an eleven-month-old child. They were concerned that he was looking weak and fatigued and was perhaps breathing a little fast. It was 9:00 P.M. During the preceding week, they had been to their family physician three times, went to another local immediate care center once, and had spoken numerous times by phone with other healthcare providers. The consensus of all involved was that the child had an ear infection that would need to run its course.

That evening in the ER the parents seemed more concerned about being reassured that nothing else was wrong. They spent a lot of energy apologizing for taking up my time and for being "alarmists". I almost fell into the trap of parental-induced complacency. The child was resting quietly in the dad's arms. For the most part, I could not find much wrong. The child looked fatigued and perhaps a bit dehydrated, but otherwise healthy. I paced the hall for a time trying to figure out what was bothering me about the child. Then it hit me: He wasn't crying, he wasn't smiling, he wasn't acting like a normal sick child, or for that matter, a normal well infant. Fifteen minutes later, I discovered this child was dying of diabetes. His blood sugar was off the charts and his blood was horribly acidic. To this day this is the youngest diabetic I have ever heard of, and at that time he was the youngest patient at Riley Children's Hospital to be put on an insulin pump.

We were able to stabilize the child and after a prolonged hospital stay, the baby was doing well, though he would require medication and multiple hospitalizations for the rest of his life. I have saved many lives, and it is incredibly rewarding. This was different. I had come within a heartbeat of reassuring this boy's parents and sending them home, which may have led them to finding their son dead in his crib the next day. It would have devastated both of us.

Another ER physician may have had the same hunch with the same results, or maybe not. I thank God every day for giving me the patience to look a little closer that evening. Later that month, I received a letter from the boy's parents filled with emotion. They poured their hearts out, thanking me for saving their child's life. I found myself suddenly needing to contact those people who played a crucial role in my medical education, which allowed me, as it had countless physicians before me, to be in a position to help a child, to save a life. Ron Galimore was the first on my list.

In an ironic twist, it just so happened that the U.S. Olympic Gymnastics Federation had recently moved their headquarters to Indianapolis. It was very easy to track Galimore down since it turned out that he now lived in the city and had become director of the U.S. Men's Olympic program.

"Hello, I'm Dr. Profeta, one of the ER physicians from St. Vincent Hospital. I'd like to speak with Mr. Ron Galimore." I always introduce myself in this way if attempting to reach someone important, because it is human nature for others to assume it must be an emergency, and so they always put me right through to them.

"Certainly sir . . . right away," came the soft feminine voice on the other end of the line.

"Hello, this is Ron . . . can I help you?"

"Ron, my name is Louis Profeta . . . you don't know me . . . I'm an ER physician here in Indianapolis and I want to tell you a story . . ."

Ron stayed quiet on the phone for the next twenty minutes while I rehashed the last eighteen years of my life, and most importantly the previous week's event. "So Ron, I'd like to take you and your wife to dinner to say thanks."

"Absolutely . . . absolutely."

I now consider Ron to be a very close friend. In 1999 I accompanied him and the men's team to China as their personal physician. It was sort of like baseball fantasy camp for me. I got to be a part of something I had strived to achieve as a younger man. And after it was all over, I realized I had no regrets. All things being equal, going to the Olympics or being a physician, hands down the latter has been and will always be more rewarding to me.

So many things shape our destinies. Why are we here, what is our role in life? In 1980 Ron Galimore became the first African-American member of the United States Olympic Gymnast Squad. However, his place in history was lost amidst the political fervor and subsequent boycott of those same games. His dedication, athleticism, and commitment to excellence became a footnote for someone else. But in 1982 a simple act of kindness lifted the spirits of a lost young man, and gave him hope and direction. In 1997 a small child lived to see many more sunsets, to dream many more dreams, and to open many more doors. I'm sure that Ron would consider this perhaps his greatest legacy.

Chapter Four

The Cosmos of the K-mart Bombing

I love fishing. I've been told that Jews don't fish, that's why God created delicatessens and lox. But I still love to fish. There is something very calming and serene about casting a line that remains very quiet on still water. I don't know if noise really scares the fish, but if you have someone, especially your children, fish with you, it's a great excuse to keep them quiet too. Everyone needs to learn how to fish; in fact it should be required in some households. I can just picture a family counseling session where the therapist looks at the group and says, "Okay...I've listened to all of you and I think I have a solution." She reaches under her desk and pulls out an old tin can full of dirt and hands it to the family. "Here are some big, juicy night crawlers. What you all need to do is just be quiet and go fishin'."

So, as my third year of medical school was winding down, that was really all I had on my mind. I wanted to take my girlfriend (now my wife) fishing and canoeing in a remote part of Canada. I also thought that a week in the wilderness might be a good way to see if we were really compatible. You see, I was planning on asking her to marry me when we returned. So, when we visited K-mart to shop for some flashlights and other fishing and camping gear, the only thing on my mind was fishing, not how to save a young girl whose frail body had just been blown apart by a bomb.

Her father, a tall distinguished man, held the door for us as we walked into the store. We nodded and smiled, my girlfriend commenting to his wife about what lovely children they had: two girls, five and about two or three, blonde, angelic and innocent. We made our way over toward the camping aisle and cruised around the store for awhile. I saw the father pushing a cart with the older of the two girls in tow. She stopped and looked at something as I turned away to talk to Sheryl. Seconds later, after rounding the corner of the aisle, out of view of the father and his child, I was lifted from my feet by an explosion. A cloud of smoke and sulfur arose to the air. Gut-wrenching, agonizing screams followed. Sheryl tried to grab me to keep me from running toward the commotion. She missed. There in the aisle, strewn with debris, this same beautiful child who greeted me at the entrance was now lying with her hand blown off, part of which was grotesquely imbedded in the roofing tile some nine feet above my head. Her eye was horribly injured, gelatinous blood trickled down her cheek, and parcels of her delicate fabric were burning. Her father lay next to her, blood and soot coated his glasses. He sat clutching his head in a look of despair that said, "My world has just ended."

At first, the young girl did not respond. The scene was a sea of utter chaos where everything was moving so quickly. I cleared some burning material from her face, smothered the flames on her shirt, and cleared open her airway. I was rewarded by a large breath and a long hard scream of the living, of a survivor. Naturally, there was panic; people were fleeing to the exits, veritable confusion. Fortunately, John Moriarty, an off-duty firefighter, showed up to help and together we did our best to try and simply bring some sense of control to a situation that bordered on pandemonium, a scene that had us just as scared, just as confused, looking around to see if we were next, forcing us to immediately come to terms with what we were witnessing.

Someone yelled that she had been shot, that it was a grenade, a bomb, a light had exploded: All sorts of theories...we just didn't know...and neither did they. We administered aide to the young girl and looked around, praying that nothing else would explode. Her parents were obviously frantic; her mother was screaming over and over, "Who did this...who did this?"

Einstein says time is relative to those experiencing it. Take into account the speed of light, the time space continuum, $E = mc2$, and... well, you get the picture. In situations of pure terror time moves at a snail's pace; one minute is twenty, an hour equals two.

I hear this from patients all the time, when their husbands or wives have suffered a heart attack or a cardiac arrest, that it took fifteen or twenty minutes for the medics to arrive, and by that time there was nothing to be done to save their family member. In actuality when the ambulance data and run sheets were reviewed, the medics almost always arrived under eight minutes. But when your loved one is dying any wait is an eternity. By my estimate, it took two days for the medics and the police to arrive and I had aged twenty years.

Before the medics showed up, we tried to collect the blown-apart fingers, placing them in a plastic bag. Towels from house-wares were used to control the bleeding; we even got a turkey baster to suction out some of the blood from her mouth. Medics finally arrived and took charge, stabilizing the young girl. A medical rescue helicopter dramatically landed in the parking lot. The white noise from the rotor quieted the crowd, offering a reprieve, a line cast on still water. She was airlifted to a local trauma center. Unfortunately, they could save neither her arm nor her eye, but she survived.

Agents from the ATF (Bureau of Alcohol, Tobacco, and Firearms) told me that it was a homemade pipe bomb that someone had sadistically placed on a shelf, in, of all things, a pump toothpaste container. The young girl had found it among some boxes of trash bags, peered inside and saw all the colorful wires, and removed the top and the rest was history. We stayed with police for a few hours, answering questions. "Why were we here? Did we see anyone suspicious? What car did we drive? Did you know the family?" Most, if not all, of the information was useless.

Fittingly, that month I was on a psychiatry rotation at Wishard

Hospital. My days were filled with, "So, sir, why are you here?"

"They made me come here just because I went to the restroom at the Subway Sandwich Shop downtown," said the little man with a flat affect and little concern.

"Why would that cause you to be committed here?" I asked, certain there must be more to the story.

"Because he used the floor in the middle of the shop to go number two," replied the nurse, not even looking up from her chart.

I had to be on rounds by 8:00 a.m., late in the morning as far as medicine goes. On other services, 5:00 or 6:00 in the morning was the norm. Around 7:00 a.m., a phone call from a local radio station woke me up. I was naively unaware what a big story this had become over the last eight hours. I quickly spoke with them about the events of the night before and said all the typical "golly, gee" garbage about how any medical student, nurse, or EMS personnel would have done the same to help out. Images of Kevin Costner in Bull Durham flashed across my brain...particularly the scene where Costner is instructing pitching sensation Tim Robbins on how best to answer the press, teaching him all of the typical baseball clichés.

"I'm just trying to do my job, be part of the team, give 100 percent, trying to contribute," says Robbins.

So, I filled them with my "oh-gosh-gee" clichés: "I'm not a hero" and "I'm sure anyone would have done the same". Then, I informed the radio personalities that I had to leave for school. They thanked me for my time, I wolfed down a pop tart and hurried to get to the medical center. By the time I had driven the thirty-minute route, I had heard my on-air interview three times. With each broadcast, the morning personalities overplayed my role dramatically. The fish, well, it just kept getting bigger. As I walked to the hospital I passed a television satellite truck outside of the Medical Sciences building. Must have made some big discovery, I thought, oblivious to the fact that they were there to see me.

I arrived at the psychiatric ward nurses' station, among the line of blank-eyed patients standing and swaying, popping Thorazine and other psychotropic drugs, or whatever it took to keep them from talking to Jesus, Satan, Martians, or the president. One of the nurses looked up and immediately embarked on the task of embarrassing the medical student, making a big deal of my involvement in the tragedy of the night before. At first I ignored it, then she held up the front page of the morning paper for all to see. All I could think was, "Oh shit, move over and give me some of those pills."

"IU Medical Student Saves Girl's Life in Bomb Explosion!" the headline read in big bold letters. Suddenly, I received my first lesson on how the world needs both heroes and villains. When it came down to it, the story was an innocent exaggeration of the facts, as most newspaper stories are. The most important exaggerated point being that I (or for that matter, we) had saved her life. We didn't: She would have lived regardless of whether I was there or not. I didn't save anyone; I just brought some sanity to an insane situation. John and I kept our cools when most everyone else was frantically out of control. The headline should have read: "Carmel Firefighter and IU Medical Student Aid Girl Injured in Bomb Blast. Child Expected to Recover." I guess it just wasn't eye-catching enough...not enough dirt, not enough drama. I read through the article, suddenly feeling somewhat uncomfortable. I went on with my daily rounds and hoped the whole thing would fade away...but then the suits showed up looking for me.

They dress in pinstripes and they carry no stethoscopes, no patient note cards, just ID tags that say things like Administrative Rep, Hospital and Corporate Communications, or Medical Liaison...fancy terms for public relations. They strongly encouraged me to take part in a press conference at the Medical Sciences building. "It would mean a lot to us and looks good for the medical center," the voiceless, faceless suits said mechanically.

I left rounds, threw on my white coat with the little IU Medical School logo, and followed the pinstripes to a conference room. Thus, by the end of the day this average medical student, who just barely passed physiology in year one, was a Warhol celebrity.

Life is funny that way. One minute you can't get a parking space at McDonald's and the next you walk into a restaurant and people are clamoring to buy you drinks. I became familiar to hearing conversations begin by, "Hey, weren't you the doctor..."

There are always consequences to being a celebrity, no matter how fleeting. I could tell it was a bone of contention for some of the other students. I guess they thought it somehow made me more competitive or allowed me some leeway on my rotations. It didn't. What it did give me was the experience of closing my eyes at night and replaying the horror and the carnage that I saw. They did not hear the screams, the sounds, the smells. They did not put severed fingers in plastic bags or lie there with a mutilated child wondering if another bomb would go off, or if someone was in the store trying to kill them. They would not have wanted to crawl into my skin, even for a second.

For weeks, every loud noise, every slammed car door, every car backfire sent me back, an amazing brief lesson into the world of the war vet. I can only imagine how innocent Israeli children responded to the barrage of suicide bombings during the Intifada.

I was still young, still very naïve, and not prepared for that kind of trauma or even more for the kind of evil that would do this to a child. I was still a kid when it came to medicine, to life and death. So with the weight of the imagery pounding in my brain, I tuned off. Someone knocked a tray of food over in the cafeteria and the explosion of dishes sent me into panic. I broke down crying and had to be escorted by my fellow students to our attending physician's office. Fortunately, as I said earlier, I was on a psychiatry rotation that month. Two weeks or so after witnessing that horror first-hand, I got my introduction into post-traumatic stress disorder, and a part of me gladly returned to just being a human being.

I had hoped all of it would die down quickly, but it didn't. There was a city council resolution proclaiming John and me as "heroes". There was a Red Cross hall of fame nominating ceremony; thank goodness they gave the award to someone else. There were the ongoing investigations, multiple news stories, and the unfortunate inability to find the person(s) responsible; all of this just kept it going. But mostly what kept it all in the psyche of the community was the shear randomness of the crime, the absolute horror in which a young girl, anyone's child, just went on a simple errand with her parents and ended up losing an eye and an arm. The emotional shock wave was devastating. Everybody saw their children, their loved ones in this crime. Everyone wanted this case solved, they needed it solved. They needed God to answer for this. As much as they needed their heroes, though, they also needed their villain. I, on the other hand, needed to get out of the city and get out of the limelight. I could imagine myself starting my residency as a young physician, doing the wrong thing, and then having my face plastered all over the paper, "K-mart Hero Found Liable for Malpractice." It seemed so feasible, so possible. So I asked my girlfriend to become my wife, and a few months later we packed our bags and left for Pittsburgh and vanished into another town and another time.

Just prior the end of medical school, about a year after the bombing, the city got its villain. It was not some bearded terrorist or some swastika-clad anarchist. It was a teenager; probably a prank, who knows? The tragic ending was that this young man killed himself just days after the initial bombing. His devastated parents notified police months later after finding items in their home that pointed to their son. His suicide suddenly made sense. I knew nothing of this family, but I felt a profound sense of loss for them, more so now that I have become a father. Their tragedy was certainly greater than anyone's, because not only was their emotionally salvageable child dead, but they were faced with the realization that he perpetrated this horrible crime. So for years I pondered over these events, wondering what they meant, why nothing good seemed to come of it. I went on with my life and relegated the K-mart bombing to a recess in my brain that would only pop out with the occasional case of nocturnal indigestion. Little did I suspect the mysticism of the universe, like a dormant tulip, was just getting ready to open up.

I got a taste of this mystic bud emerging a few years back when I got a strange call. The Carmel City Council, or some similar organization, wanting to honor me in a "Parade of Carmel Heroes".

"Wow...what an honor," I said to the lady on the other end of the line. I assumed it was to thank me for all the patients I had cared for in my years of service at Carmel St. Vincent Hospital. I was wrong again. I guess that stuff wasn't sexy enough. As it turned out the master of ceremonies was one Richard Jewell. You might remember him as that poor guy who was a suspect in the Olympic Park bombing. He was the security guard who, by moving the crowd back, almost certainly saved many lives only to be later accused of the crime for which Eric Rudolph is now serving the rest of his life in jail for committing.

This simple guy went from national hero to a mistaken national villain to a forgotten cog in the media machinery. His whole life was scrutinized and torn apart by an overzealous media that, to this day, has offered very little in the way of apology. A good, honest man who lived and cared for his mother. I still choke up just thinking of him. He is a remarkable and tragic figure in American History.

Well, I guess someone at the Carmel Council felt it was time to honor Richard Jewell for his heroism and somehow that whole bombing thing triggered memories of an earlier event in our city, another time and another bombing. My response was easy, "No way!" Then John called. By that time he had become a high-ranking official in the Carmel Fire Department. He was being pressured by 'the suits' to be in the parade.

"Oh yeah, I remember them," I told him. "I met them at the medical center about twelve years ago. What are they calling them these days; public relations, corporate communications?"

"Something like that," he laughed. He told me even though he was being strongly encouraged to participate, he wouldn't do it if I didn't. I thought on it for about a day then called and told the suit that I would take part in the parade, ride in the convertible and wave to the crowd on one condition. I wanted my wife and kids to ride with me. My kids had never even heard the story, and when I told them the 'G-rated' version, they thought it was kind of cool that I was there to help.

It was obvious that they were proud of me and it kind of warmed my heart to know that I was a hero to them; much like my dad is to me. So we tossed out candy to the crowd, waved and said hello to our friends and answered the calls of children who had never heard of the event of years past and in the end it was great closure to a painful part of my life. Once again my world had started to come full circle. I was with my own children, holding them tight, watching them toss candy, oblivious to the real sequence of events that placed us in the convertible with the magnetic signs that read "Dr. Profeta, Carmel Hero". It was a purely innocent and joyful experience, one that easily replaced my memories of that day. So now when I hear, "Hey…weren't you the doc that…" my mind conjures up images of smiling children catching candy and waving to my family through the cobblestone streets of a small town, not a bad trade.

In a newspaper interview, Richard Jewell related to the local media that when he first got the call to be the grand marshal for the parade of heroes, he thought it was a joke…no one had honored him like this. Well Carmel, Indiana did. I am proud of them for that.

Richard Jewell will always be one of my heroes. He did his job and walked upright when the whole world was wrong. I'm grateful for the role he played to protect the lives of strangers. Richard Jewell restored my faith in humanity. I am grateful to God for giving me eyes to see that we are all linked, that we all have a responsibility to each other. If our deeds and our actions drum up images of heroism in others, then maybe it's not so bad. People need heroes to remind them of the human potential and how our hearts and souls can truly shine at a moment's notice.

So now it seemed as if life had come full circle. The ends were linked. The ring was set. The finality was the parade, time with my kids, Richard Jewell. This door on my life was now closed and neatly packaged on a shelf somewhere in my memory cabinet. But once again, I was mistaken.

The early version of this book had been in publication for about a year and it had done quite well. The reviews were beyond my expectations and I was thrilled that people seemed to connect to it. A friend of my folks approached me and asked if I could give him a copy to give to Erin. Erin is the name of the young girl in the bombing. I was hesitant to do this, I'm not sure why, but I gave over a copy anyway.

Unbeknownst to me, the twentieth anniversary of the K-mart bombing had arrived. I was working in the ER on a not-so-busy shift. "Dr. Profeta, one of the local television stations is here to do a story, do you have some time?" The public relations representative, dressed in a fine pressed suit, politely asked. Over the years I had become somewhat of a local expert on community public health issues, things like falls, frostbite, heat exhaustion, etc, and appeared frequently on radio and TV, so this was not an odd request.

Certain that it was about the impending swine flu epidemic I responded, "Yeah, sure...but give me a second to brush up on the CDC recommendations for swine flu so I don't say anything stupid or incorrect."

"This is not about swine flu…it's about the K-mart bombing." He smiled knowingly. A shapely young anchorwoman appeared by his side. She clutched a copy of my book as she leaned over the counter and smiled at me.

"Dr. Profeta," she chimed in. "We are doing a story on the K-mart bombing, it's the twentieth year anniversary of the event. We talked to the girl's parents and they asked that we talk with you. You see Erin went to college and is now a physical therapist. She helps young children who are sick and disabled……" For a brief second I actually envisioned a five year old girl in college.

"And….." I interrupted, knowing another cosmic link in the chain was about to be added.

"Well….and….Erin works in this very same hospital now…just two floors up. She just started in the children's pavilion." She calculated her pause to gauge my reaction.

My heart seemed to hover between beats. I had really only one mental image of Erin and it was not one that I was anxious to revisit. But I really kind of wanted to see her, see what she had become and take a glimpse of where she was headed. So with cameras in tow, and with the blessing of her parents, we walked the corridor to where she worked. The lights flipped on and we surprised Erin at work.

"Erin….this is Doctor Profeta." This young shattered body had grown to a tall, beautiful, confident young woman, more whole with one arm than most are with two. I was humbled and proud all rolled into one slobbering idiot.

So the television ran the story with clips spanning the gap from that long ago time in K-mart to our not-so-by-chance meeting in the hospital. I watch myself age twenty years, go bald and get kind of fat. I saw the world flash in front of my aging eyes and I smiled at the thoughts of where I have been and where I am headed and what I have learned.

This whole cosmic spiritual circle is nothing of the kind. It is an endless series of links of a chain that bind us all together. It is magical, mystical, often tragic and wondrous at the same time. It is everything. It is amazing and it is perfect.

Chapter Five

Buddy, Can You Spare a Liver?

There is an old Yiddish saying: "No one with money deserves it." Most physicians will extend that to: "No doctor deserves to be more respected or successful than me." That feeling is especially pervasive in academic medicine, where the clashes of egos are fought with the enthusiasm of a full-blown jihad. But there is one person whom I can truly say I don't, in any sense of the word, envy his success or his accomplishments. That person is my friend, Joe Tector. In his field of medicine, every operation he performs leaves someone dead.

What if I told you that someone tossing dirty ashes from a charcoal grill in 1985 helped save the life of a small child some sixteen years later? Could you make the connection? I am constantly in awe of how a simple act, the turn of a dial, can have such a profound impact on our world. Albert Einstein hangs out a few more years in Nazi Germany, and as a Jew, he perishes in Auschwitz, and in all likelihood the very computer on which I type this story does not exist. You see, it was his basic work in math and physics that led to the invention of many everyday items such as personal computers, cell phones, and television. Or, Alois and Klara Hitler don't meet, perhaps never go out for beer and a braut, and six million more people are contributing to the beautiful mosaic of this world.

But . . . what if those two girls living upstairs had not chosen to empty their old grill over the balcony at the precise time that I was sitting directly below them and working on my Tandy 1000 home computer? What if they had not accidentally blanketed me with a heavy dose of Mount St. Helen's ash that shorted out my two-tone screen and dot-matrix printer? Would that child still be alive sixteen years later? Because it was my rash of obscene expletives that made Joe to step out of his apartment to see what the commotion was about, and it was the friendship formed by that chance meeting that would work a miracle years later.

After he helped dust me off, shook the soot from my stack of papers, and had a good laugh, Joe glanced down and noticed that I was working diligently on complex immunology homework from the quintessential textbook on the subject by Roitt. By then, I was a senior in college waiting to hear if I was going to be admitted to medical school. Joe was a junior pre-med student, and we hit it off immediately. There are those people that walk into your life who, after just a few moments, you know that you will be friends for life: Joe was one of them. We had absolutely nothing, while having absolutely everything, in common. He was Catholic; I was Jewish. He was quiet, calculating, and somewhat reserved in public, while quite the opposite in private. I was loud, opinionated, and impulsive. He grew up a son of privilege: private schools, tennis courts, and swimming pools. His father was a famous heart surgeon; in fact, he was one of the early pioneers of redo-cardiac bypass surgery, the artificial heart, and heart transplantation. My father sold insurance and was the first to graduate from college in his family. He had the benefit of his father's experience in medicine. Me, I was just cruising through school by the skin of my teeth, hoping not to screw up while trying to find guidance where I could. However, I faced little expectation on the part of my parents to succeed. Joe had to walk in the footsteps of a giant.

Having been a solid 'C' student in high school with an average SAT score, it was a miracle that I was even accepted into college. So, when I decided to pursue an honors biology degree and go pre-med, my parents did not hide their skepticism and suggested that I take business classes . . . just in case. Joe, however, was expected to carry the torch of the family, to set the stage for the ongoing family legacy of super-achievement. My folks would've been contented if I married a nice Jewish girl and didn't do something stupid to get myself killed before giving them some grandkids. Joe was under much more pressure to succeed, though he would never admit it.

I have to be honest; in the early years, I didn't think Joe had what it took to be a physician. His quiet way and his calm public demeanor hid the fire, the overdrive inside of him. One day, we were sitting around and Joe mentioned how he planned to get a PhD in immunology, do a residency in general surgery, a fellowship in transplantation, and learn how to do liver and other organ transplants, while at the same time, pursue research into xenografts (animal organs transplanted into human recipients). He might as well have told me he planned to run for president, since it seemed as likely to happen from my perspective. I even notated his vision in an immunology book and gave it to him in 1985, fairly certain that little of his over-the-top plan would come to fruition. Well, he left out a fellowship in critical care, becoming the head of organ transplantation, being the first surgeon to do an intestinal transplant in the state of Indiana, and the first to do a multivisceral transplant in the state (liver, pancreas, and small and large intestines), and single-handedly to increase the number of liver transplants in Indiana from about 20 per year to more than 180. Thus, he was able to save the lives of hundreds of people who would otherwise have died awaiting organs in a state that was less than aggressive in this pursuit.

Let me put time into perspective: I started medical school in 1986, Joe in 1987. I was in private practice by 1993; it took Joe until 1999. He spent nearly seven more years than me in school and fellowship programs. We were both so busy that we essentially allowed three years to pass without seeing each other, then another six until our next meeting. Sure, we would talk on the phone maybe once every six months or so, mundane stuff full of "how's it goings?"

Understand this about residency: we, just like all residents, were damn busy. We essentially knew what the other was doing during these years: Like every resident physician, we were locked away in some rotation, doing scutt work, reading, studying for boards, and finding our way through the labyrinth of resident training. So, unless something spectacular or out of the ordinary happened, like growing a third eye, or hitting the lottery, we knew exactly what the other was doing, because a thousand miles away, we were doing the same damn thing.

"Hey, Joe . . . how's it going?"

"Hey, Louis . . . what's up?"

"Finished residency . . . and you?"

"Getting a PhD in immunology, right now. Can I give you a call back after I'm done?"

"Yeah, no problem."

So it did not surprise me that out of the blue I got a call from Joe.

"Hey, what's up?"

"I'm in Jacksonville, Florida."

"What are you doing in Florida?"

"A fellowship in transplant surgery."

"Did you just start?"

"No, finishing up . . . I've been here two years."

"Oh."

"Hey, I'm coming to Indiana to interview for a job."

"Why? You're not from here."

"Because you Hoosiers aren't using your livers. I keep flying in from Jacksonville and taking them. I figured I might as well look at the possibility of setting up shop. Can I stay with you for a few months while the kids finish school and Kelly sells the house?"

"No problem. Give me a call when you get here."

So, Joe moved in and I made sure the kitchen was stocked with plenty of popcorn and Mountain Dew, staples for most busy surgeons. My rambunctious and moderately distracting sons were at times a burden, especially after a heavy day of organ harvesting. Joe entertained them by playing games. His favorite was Coma. Whoever played coma the longest was the winner. The rules: you had to hold really still, not make a sound, and not move; it was brilliant. Anytime I want some peace and quiet, I play it with my kids. The winner gets a dollar.

My home was a dose of reality for Joe, a chance to be brought back to earth, whether he liked it or not. One second, he is saving the life of a dying child and the next, my second son is telling slightly portly Joe that he looks like 'Fat Bastard' from Austin Powers. He would go from praise and accolades from an envious medical establishment only to get trash talk from a first-grader. But Joe put up with my kids' ribbing. After all, it's hard to laugh hysterically and discipline a child at the same time. Eli now shows him the respect Joe deserves—he calls him 'Uncle Fat Bastard' behind his back.

You have to have a sense of humor to be an ER physician, and more so to be a transplant surgeon, or else the death will overwhelm you. Joe once devised a good-natured revenge plot on a lactation consultant who embarrassed him during the birth of one of his kids. Unbeknownst to the innocent nurse, he recommended her to consult on a cross-dressing male transvestite who wore a pink tutu and was trying to breast-feed a plastic doll. Her surprise was understandable, as was her indignation upon walking in to see the patient. He had to go before the surgery chief on that one. I always wonder how someone does the type of job Joe does, how horrible and wonderful at the same time. I once asked him about how he closes the body of the deceased child who has donated the liver; he dropped his head and you could see the pain in his face. "I close that wound with more care than a plastic surgeon, and care for the body as if it were my own living child. I am well aware of the profound despair on the part of the dead child's family, and the responsibility and the gift they have given my patient."

Therein lies the character of Joe and why I am so fortunate to have him as my friend; it is also why the world is that much better to be treaded by the likes of him.

Months passed, and Joe's wife and kids moved to Indianapolis and took refuge in a small apartment until his house was built. They spent many a night at our home, so as to avoid their cramped quarters filled with three dogs, two birds, three kids, and a pile of medical books, dirty clothes, and journal articles.

It was usual, then or now, for Joe to be gone thirty-six to forty-eight hours straight, maybe catching one or two hours of sleep here and there between cases. His wife and kids, as well as many husbands and wives of physicians (including mine), are the unsung heroes. In all practical sense, she is a single mother forced to share her partner with so many sick and needy people. In many instances, it is with him being there and not being there at the same time—lost in a world of organ procurement, cell phones, pagers, and 24-hour phone inquiries. In Joe's case, his wife Kelly has the very important job of helping her husband stay focused during the long and grueling cases. It is usual for him and the other transplant physician to go untold hours operating on the same patient; one will break scrub and the other will continue, each giving the other a break as the hours drag on.

It has become somewhat of the norm for Joe and me to spend many hours talking on the phone, picking each other's brain for advice on medicine, on parenting, and on how just to live sanely. Since we are keenly aware from whence each of us came, we don't have much of a problem figuring where each of us is headed, so we try to make sure each other's airbags are operational and our seatbelts are fastened. So, when Joe stopped by the ER around two in the morning to wind down from one of his cases, just to say hello, neither of us had any idea that it would save the life of a small child a few months later.

"Hey, Josh . . . Josh!" I shouted. Josh Careskey is a pediatric surgeon who works in our community hospital, and a damn good one, too. "I want you to meet a friend of mine that stopped by to say hello." He glanced at his watch, confused for a second.

"Josh, he's a liver transplant surgeon at the medical center, and my old college roommate. He did a case tonight and was just stopping by on his way home." Josh laughed and nodded.

"Josh . . . Joe Tector. Joe, this is Josh Careskey, one of our finest 'ped' surgeons." They acknowledged each other and shook hands. Joe swayed nervously in place. "Josh, let me brag for a second. Joe is one of the new transplant surgeons at the medical center, here to increase the number of transplants, especially in kids. He's even hoping to get an intestinal transplant program started in the state."

"Really?" Josh asked inquisitively. "Does that actually work . . . transplanting just the intestines into a kid? They do okay with all the anti-rejection medications and stuff?"

"We've done a few in Florida and had great results," Joe responded. They talked a little more and Josh went on to see some kid in the ER who needed his appendix removed. Joe hung out for a while, and then headed home.

A few months later, that brief middle-of-the-night visit would give a child a chance of surviving into adulthood. Josh had been called to see a young boy with severe abdominal pain. He took the four-year-old child to the operating room, anticipating the child was suffering from a twisted or blocked piece of intestine. Instead, he found something horrible. The entire intestinal tract had been strangulated; the blood supply had been cut off, and boy's entire bowel was dead. We call this 'dead gut' or 'dead bowel'; a small section alone can be fatal, but the entire intestinal tract was a death sentence. Josh prepared to close the child and tell the family that the young boy would certainly die in the next day or so. Then, he recalled something . . . a name . . . a chance meeting.

"Get me Dr. Tector on the phone from the med center; he's a

liver or transplant surgeon."

Joe immediately called back while Josh was still hovering over the dead gut—the child wide open in the OR. "Resect the dead gut," Joe said. "Put in a central line and a g-tube, then send him to me . . . let's see what we can do."

A few hours later, Joe was faced with the daunting task of saving this dying child. Meanwhile, Josh prepared to go out of town, leaving the young boy in Joe's care. Twenty-four hours later, Joe obtained a donor from California and transplanted the entire intestinal tract from a brain-dead child into this young boy.

The child is now eight years old, in school, and eats the same normal junk food that any child his age enjoys. More important, he is alive.

When Josh returned a few weeks later, I congratulated him. "On what?" he asked.

"That kid you sent to Joe; he transplanted a whole intestinal tract and he's doing great . . . what, you didn't know?" Josh was floored but elated. He had not checked his voicemail and had no idea that the child was still alive, let alone survived the transplant. His voice cracked on the phone. "Oh my God, I'm going to cry," he said. "It's truly a miracle, a miracle."

So, in 1985 two coeds shorted out my computer when they cleaned their grill. In 2002, a young boy survived what would otherwise have been a fatal complication.

We can only imagine how simple acts and twists of fate send us down one road or the other in life, but I know I have never been more grateful to have been covered in soot. There is a funny thing about time and true friendship: You can be separated by miles and years, but once you are back together, all is the same. You can pick up from where you left off and talk like you've never missed a day. That is, unless the reality of those missing years brings an unnecessary sense of loss instead of a sense of accomplishment for time well spent. I now understand all of those poems by Frost and Wordsworth and whoever else lamented over the passing of their youth, of quieter days.

One moment, Joe and I are young college students getting into bar fights, pushing the envelope of decency, and praying we get into medical school. The next he's taking the liver from a brain-dead child and putting it into another, and I'm telling a son that Mom or Dad has died. I think we both look at each other and wonder, "How in the hell did we get here?" It is beyond surreal; it approaches mystical proportions. And when we sit on my back porch and watch our kids play together, look up at the immensity of a starry night, it just seems to make sense; things just seem right . . . like there's a plan.

Chapter Six

Stay for Breakfast, Mr. Brown

I liked him immediately when I first met him. I can't explain why. There was just something very peaceful, honest, and humble in his demeanor. He was covered with paint and drywall dust that matched his grey hair. Dressed in work clothes, it was obvious that he was a laborer, probably in construction. He told me that he had retired from Allison or Cummings Engine—I can't recall which, or maybe it was Chrysler. He had a cut on his hand that needed sutures. We carried on with small talk as I anesthetized his hand and cleaned his wound. I slowly placed the sutures so as to have more time to talk with him. There was something about him. He calmed my spirit. He told me that he did home repair, drywall, and painting to help pay the bills and so he could buy nice things for his grandchildren. It just so happened I needed my garage painted and some drywall repair. He gave me his card and we set a time for him to come out and give a bid on the project. The quote was ridiculously fair; my wife liked him and he was hired on the spot. Since we were leaving on vacation, we gave him a key to the garage, completely trusting that this man whom we hardly knew would take good care of our home.

When we returned, the garage was nicer than my house; I wanted to move the couch and TV out there but my wife drew the line there. After that, we told him not to take any jobs for the near future since he was going to be working at our home for a while. He painted the kids' rooms, the hallways, and the wood trim. He was slow and meticulous, a rare breed of handyman who took excessive pride in his work, paid attention to detail, sharpened all edges, and straightened all lines. We shared sodas on the back porch. He would talk with reverence about his wife, his children, and especially his daughter who was due to have twins. He smiled so broadly when he spoke about his family and the pending birth of his grandchildren that it moved air. He seemed able to fix anything from a door hinge to simple electrical wiring to a broken window. I imagine that as a father he could have fixed broken hearts, hurt feelings, and injured pride with the same degree of skill. He got a kick out of my young sons, and they seemed to take to him. My oldest son Max would sit with him and tell in detail just how he wanted his room painted. He liked Mr. Brown, who even let him help out a bit. He soon became a fixture around the house, and if he had only eaten a bagel that morning, he might be alive today.

All of us walk through life with 'what if' stories. And I know I've been harping on this theme, but it's essential to my search for answers. So, what if we had been there five minutes early, or two minutes late? What if I had been driving with him, or had been eating lunch with her that day? What if I had been sitting there, or walking the same way back to the office? What if? I think 'what if' stories are not so much near misses: they are celestial slaps upside the head from God. They are the Friday-at-noon civil defense alarms of life that jolt us back to reality. For others, unfortunately, they are tragedies that leave us asking why them, not me; why him, not her? I don't believe in fate per se. I think there are just so many of us moving around so quickly that it is inevitable that on occasion we collide with each other, with nature, or just with ourselves at times. God gives us the rule book: a mind, heart, and soul; the rest is up to us.

'What if' questions are the source of so much despair in the ER, and the cause of so much grief in our daily lives, that we should wear a Pavlovian shock collar to jolt us every time those two words pop in our heads. What if I had only insisted he come to the ER for his chest pain, what if I stuck to my guns and took away the keys—what if, what if, and what if?

When I was in fourth grade my family and I were driving back from Chicago on I-65 in northern Indiana just outside of Monticello. Dad and Mom were in the front seat. My grandma sat in the middle seat, while my sisters played with their Barbie dolls in the back seat. I lay in the back of our white Ford ranch wagon, tucked in amongst the luggage. It was raining very hard, and for a while, thick greasy rain coated the windshield, and then it suddenly stopped. The sky was dark with an undulating deep green canopy of clouds, and the air was very still. I stared out the window, noticing how one patch of sky a few hundred yards off to the side of the car was churning about. It was so odd and beautiful at the same time, just one patch on still sky. The next moment, a monster in the form of a giant tornado dropped from the sky perhaps 300 yards from the side of our car. I screamed and pointed at our soon-to-be executioner; my family erupted in panic and the car shook from the deafening roar. We were the last car to make it past Monticello on

I-65. The tornado devastated the town, and if I recall correctly, numerous people were killed. "What if we had left the hotel thirty seconds later?" I ask myself each time I recall this episode. The answer: we might just have well been hit by a truck at the toll road. We ruminate and we ponder on these near misses ad nauseam, and the reality is we will never really know, or should know.

Part of me believes that Mr. Brown died because he didn't eat a bagel. He was not quite finished with the paint job in my son's room; there was a bit of trim molding to touch up, but he had to get to Missouri or Illinois or somewhere to do some painting for a relative; who, in turn, was going to repair his personal home computer. He thus had all of his paint supplies, mineral spirits, and turpentine in the back of the van. He asked cautiously if he could get paid, even though he had only a small amount of work left to do.

"Of course," I said, having no doubt he would finish the job at a later date, no doubt whatsoever. I paid him about $500; he stopped at my bank, cashed the check, and hopped onto I-70 heading toward Illinois. He slowed down for a traffic jam on the interstate and was promptly hit from behind by a huge semi-truck that had failed to notice the slowed-down traffic. The van exploded and Mr. Brown died instantly: He was burned beyond recognition.

What if Mr. Brown had eaten the bagel or accepted the cup of coffee that I had offered him that morning? The truck most certainly would have been in front of him, and perhaps then this accident would not have happened. Or, perhaps the truck would have run into a family of six coming back from Chicago, killing them instantly, including two little girls playing with Barbies in the back seat. I have no doubt that Mr. Brown would not have wanted to change places with that family; he certainly would have preferred that God take him instead.

Though we hardly knew him, Sheryl and I went to his funeral, where we met his family. We learned he was a decorated Vietnam veteran and a good, honest churchgoing man, who loved his family dearly. My oldest son Max wrote Mr. Brown a note telling him how much he liked his new room. If you visit our house, you will notice a small amount of wood trim that has not yet been painted. The lines are simple and straight. It is an honest piece of wood, a noon alarm, a reminder of how thankful I am to be on this earth, and also how thankful I am to have known this gentle man even for a short time.

But I have figured out the answer to some 'what if' questions, though. What if we never learned from our near misses, our noontime civil defense alarms? What if we failed to appreciate a gentle moment, the smile of a child, or the feeling of fresh air upon our faces? What if we failed to tell our friends and family how much we love them? Well, that would be a real tragedy.

Chapter Seven

"There's a Cockroach in My Ear"

Now, before you think it's funny, trust me, it isn't. Anyone who has ever had a cockroach or any other bug in their ear can tell you it is horrifically painful. Picture that little insect with its sharp, hairy claws, replete with hooks and nails to allow it to climb up vertical surfaces, scraping and ripping at your eardrum. Now you get the picture. There you are, asleep on your couch without a care in the world, and the little vermin climbs up your shirt, across your hair, and sees a nice little tunnel to snuggle in. Next thing you know you feel like someone has driven an ice pick into your ear. So when the woman came into the ER with the chief complaint of a cockroach in her ear, I rushed backed to her room, ready to alleviate her discomfort. Instead of finding an ear full of insect, I found a can full of worms.

"Quick, get it out!" she yelled, grabbing at her ear. "It's a cockroach, it crawled in my ear." I grabbed the otoscope from the wall along with a set of alligator forceps. "Calm down, slow your breathing…I'll get it out." I laid her back on the bed and turned her head to the side, adjusted the light, and prepared to come face to face with the vile bag of segmented, antennae-bearing, bacteria-laden, kingdom animalia, phylum insecta. To my surprise, all I saw was the pearly white luminescence of a pristine eardrum glistening on the end of a completely clear ear canal. There was not even a small ball of wax present.

"Uhhhhh, it's this ear, right?" I asked, backing away from her head briefly.

"Yes, yes!" she screamed. "Get it out…get it out."

I slowly approached her ear again, looking around to see if

maybe it had crawled out prior to my exam. I looked around her scalp to see if maybe I missed shingles or something else. I slowly pulled her ear back and again looked deep into her ear canal. Again, I was met with nothing but a perfect, non-inflamed, completely benign, normal, everyday, good old working eardrum. "Ma'am, I've got good news; there is nothing there. I bet it already crawled out." I figured that she would be completely comforted by this fact, but I was wrong.

"Listen, you idiot; there is a cockroach in my ear...where did you go to medical school? How hard is it for you to see that there is a cockroach in my ear? You are not looking in the right place, dammit. Get me someone else who knows what they are doing."

I maintained my cool and avoided the trap of getting angry at my patient. "Ma'am, let me look again. Perhaps I missed something, but it's not like it can hide from me in there. The ear is like looking into a thimble; either something is in there or it's not...but let me check again." I slowly looked into her ear, spending a good deal of time so as not to appear rushed, and rattled off the anatomy: "The canal looks great, no rash, no lesions...good-looking ear drum, no fluid, pearly white...that's good...great light, great...nope...nope...looks really good, ma'am. Great news, I think it probably crawled out."

"You may be the worse doctor I have ever met...how you cannot see the cockroach in my ear is beyond me. I want to talk to your boss now! You're a moron."

That's when I said it...it couldn't be helped. "Ma'am, lay back and let me look again." I turned her head and looked into her other ear.

"What the hell are you looking there? It's the other ear, you idiot," she responded.

"Ma'am, I'm just making sure it didn't crawl through to the other side," I said with a big, sarcastic smile on my face. With that she jumped out of the bed and stormed out of the ER. A few days later I received a copy of the patient complaint from hospital administration called in by the patient. It described me as being condescending and incompetent, and not taking this patient's concern seriously.

My dear friend Joe always tells me, "If you never say it, you don't have to apologize for it." I truly believe that God has a sense of humor. If he didn't, why would he have created the anteater, the dung beetle, reality TV, and the 'thigh-master'? I think we are occasionally thrown curve balls in our life just to see how we will respond. I am sure God would have preferred that I put my arm around this woman and do everything in my power to turn her anger into comfort, her oppositional behavior into love. I am certain that he would have wanted me to embrace the golden rule, love thy neighbor and that whole do unto other mantra. And if I had to do it all over again, I would have taken that path…no, come to think of it…who am I kidding? I would have said the same thing…the letter of apology was worth it.

Chapter Eight

A Christmas Story

I grew up on the east side of Indianapolis. We were the only Jewish family on that side of town, and it was far from a welcoming experience. I knew at a very early age that I was different, and the neighborhood kids let me know it from the outset. In the late 1960s and early 1970s, our city was less than culturally diverse. While we were still feeling the pains and the turmoil around the deaths of Martin, Malcolm, Bobby, and Jack, we still did not welcome a sense of cultural diversity into our small corner of the world. I recalled being called "Christ killer", "Jew boy", "kike", and other anti-Semitic slurs from children my same age, who were only at fault for being born in an era of ethnic bigotry.

I remember with great clarity the first time I met an African-American child in my school, a product of busing to integrate our school system and bring a sense of community balance. I recall two young Vietnamese refugees who somehow found their way to our grade school, exposing us to the realities of war and bringing the realization that there was a whole world of non-English speaking people out there. And I remember thinking that, with each of these new foreign faces, somehow they would take the pressure off of me, but it never happened.

Christmas would roll around and my parents would beg me not to tell the other children that Santa was not real, which was like asking a precocious kid like me not to touch the chocolate cake. Besides, I had to teach a lesson to all those who called me names and teased me about not eating the ham sandwiches and pigs in a blanket at lunch.

"Your mom and dad hide your presents in the closet, in the

trunk of the car, or under their beds, and then bring them out when you're asleep . . . you idiots!"

"You're just jealous because Santa Claus doesn't come to your house 'cause you're a Jew." This was usually accompanied by profound crying, a quick run home, and a choreographed "you killed Jesus" on their return.

So, as a fifth grader at the Christmas program, I finally had enough of standing in the choir and singing *Away in a Manger,* *Silent Night,* or *Little Drummer Boy.* I stood in proud defiance, with my arms crossed and my lips sealed for the whole school to see. After the program I sat with my father and the principal locked away in her office, and I cried from years of the deep pain for always being excluded—only to be met with a look of understanding from both the principal and my father. From that day forward, school was forever changed for me.

Sometimes it takes one encounter to change a person's perspective, to shake their spiritual foundations. The tragedy of 9/11 is a perfect example about how one act can permanently alter the way we view the world. In 1993, one patient made me wonder if perhaps we are all really on the same plane worshiping the same God, with reservations in the same heaven.

It was November 30; this girl was beautiful and late in her pregnancy. Unfortunately she had not felt the baby kick for a while, so she came to the ER where an ultrasound reading showed the infant was dead. The profoundly distraught mother was taken to labor and delivery, where she gave birth to a stillborn fetus. Immediately thereafter she became suddenly ill and was sent back to the ER. Her respirations increased, her oxygen level and blood pressure dangerously dropped off, and she broke out in a fine rash. Her lungs filled with fluid, her heart rate soared, and she lapsed into a coma—a victim of life-threatening septic shock. We gave her twenty liters of fluid and administered potent blood pressure-supporting medications at critical rates in an attempt to maintain a blood pressure that hovered at about 50 over zero. Her lungs shut down, her kidneys stopped functioning, and in less than six hours this fine rash had formed large blood-filled blisters covering nearly her entire body, confirming her diagnosis of sepsis due to a deadly infection of Neisseria meningitis. Her baby had died because of this nonselective assassin and now it was taking her mom, and we knew from the literature that the mortality rate was nearly 100 percent for a patient with her degree of illness. So my fellow resident Bill and I took over her care and awaited her death.

It happened that she was assigned to our service for the ensuing month. We had just finished our November ER rotation in this small community hospital and were now, as third-year residents from the University of Pittsburgh, next to take over the hospital's six-bed Intensive Care Unit (ICU). Thus, she went from the ER to being in our charge in the ICU.

She was so ill that we literally had to sit at her bedside day after day, making minuscule adjustments in her ventilator and her medications, just hoping we could maybe beat the odds and help bring her back from the dead. Her body grotesquely swelled from all the fluid; large patches of skin blackened and died. Her eyes and skin yellowed from liver failure and her coma deepened, but somehow she still maintained a trace of a blood pressure. We tried high doses of steroids, and an experimental antibody serum flown in especially for her. We hit the library looking for something we could try, but all signs pointed to a fatal outcome. We placed her on a modified type of dialysis, taking off just enough toxins and fluids to sustain her life, and days remarkably became weeks. A CT scan of her brain looked surprisingly good, and an EEG showed that somewhere deep, deep inside this ill woman, her brain still worked, calling out, "My soul has not left; tell my mother that I'm still here and I'm not ready to leave."

For three weeks she languished, hovering between this world and the next. She lay casket-still, the only perceptible movement was the rise and the fall of her mechanical breathing, and it became clear that if she didn't make a move toward recovery, she would probably die around Christmas.

I worked Christmas Eve, as I have every year since medical school. I am keenly aware of the importance the holiday holds for my non-Jewish friends, and I always am quick to take the reins and volunteer. But let's also be realistic. If you've seen all the latest movies and are not too keen on Chinese food, there is not too much for Jews to do on Christmas Day anyway. I also liked the notion that if the whole 'Jesus' thing was true, I'm sure he'd much rather I was attending to the sick and downtrodden on his birthday than going gaga over another new sweater. So, every year, we congregate on Christmas in cinemas, Hunan and Szechwan restaurants, and the local hospitals all across America. For me this Christmas Eve was different, though. There was not a sense of anticipation but of dread that she would die on this night, and this sacred holiday would forever link her family to her death.

It was very quiet in her room that night; the radiator was lined with cards, unlit prayer candles, flowers, and scattered gilded-framed pictures of the Virgin Mary. Her family lay sleeping in the ICU waiting room, maintaining a Christmas vigil, no visions of sugar plums for them. I walked softly around the room, checking the lines, the monitors, and looking for signs of change. I meandered around the trinkets, touching the candles, reading the cards, smelling the flowers, and pausing at a picture of the Virgin Mary.

"You know . . . I'm Jewish, just like you, and I don't know if you listen to my prayers too . . . but if you have an 'in' with God somehow, the time is now to step up and help this poor girl, 'cause we don't have much left to offer at our end . . . if you know what I mean." And with that the air conditioner violently kicked on and scared the living crap out of me. After I composed myself and turned to make sure no one noticed, I laughed and then turned toward the young woman just in time to see it—she moved her hand and opened her eyes, and my own heart nearly stopped.

She lived, and although she needed lots of surgeries, skin grafting, dialysis, and a subsequent kidney transplant, she went back to her life, back to her family and those who loved her, and lived to celebrate many more Christmas days with them.

Now before you think that I turned in my Jewish Community Membership Card and joined the YMCA, trust me, it didn't happen. But I do believe I experienced a deep spiritual connection, a brief closeness with God in a manner I didn't expect. So many times in my career I have been on the razor's edge of a catastrophe, and I had a feeling that God was helping me out, helping me to focus, calming my soul during chaos and crisis. In this situation, though, I was not asking for help or guidance for me. I was comfortable, even calm in knowing that I had done everything possible. The lines were in, medications were flowing, and all the tubes were in the right place. It was out of my hands, and the only real task left was to surrender to a higher power. It just did not feel right for me on Christmas Eve to pray to the God I knew, in the way I was accustomed. I was again a Jewish boy on the stage of a Christmas play. Only this time I was playing the part of the voice of a dying woman, pleading to the mother of God she knew, on the day that was profoundly special and sacred to her, in the only way I could—with frank, in-your-face candor, arms crossed in defiance . . . and I think she listened.

Chapter Nine

Maria, Maria . . . I Believe

There you have it. I believe in God. Mind you that it's not without a slew of questions, like the Holocaust, Rwanda, Stalin, and the Red Sox over my Yankees. But when it boils down to it, the basic concept of a divine presence, a force for good and humanity, I believe. I must admit that this has not come easy, and I certainly am not like those reborn types who always seem to have a smile, where everything is Jesus this and the lord that, though I am absolutely envious of their peace of mind and the way they go through life with their conviction of faith guiding them. No, I am different in this regard. I am deeply affected by the world around me. I fight and argue with God as much as a teenager with his father. I love God, I curse God, I thank him, and I blame him. I am an adolescent when it comes to my faith, and no matter what I do that does not change. Each year during the holy holiday of Yom Kippur, I tell God I am sorry for all my transgressions, and I apologize and promise not to repeat them, knowing damn well I will be here next year asking forgiveness for the same offenses. "Where does that leave me?" is the question I always seem to ask myself. Does God like me? No, not love me . . . does he like me? I have many relatives that I love, but I don't necessarily like them. Am I the obnoxious cousin who, when God checks his call-waiting, looks over to Moses and says, "It's Profeta again . . . don't answer it." I like to think that's not the case, but I suspect otherwise.

I think God is the AAA of humanity: He gives you the roadmap but you still have to drive through life. You can avoid the traffic congestion and roadwork if you want, but ultimately it's up to you which direction you go. But in my life, in my career, he has shown himself to me so often that I have no doubt as to his existence. I just wish I could have believed it earlier.

I was working the nightshift. It was about 2:00 A.M. and fairly slow. Suddenly it hit me, like a blow to the chest . . . a kind of knowing. I looked up from my paperwork and said to no one in particular, "My Aunt Maria just died."

"What?" one of the nurses asked, peering up from her charting.

"Uhhhh . . . what's the number for the hospice? My Aunt Maria just died." I fumbled around with the receiver, dropping it twice before getting it to my ear. I dialed the number to New Hope Hospice Center, where my dear aunt had languished for the last few months with metastatic colon cancer.

"St. Vincent Hospice, may I help you?" the soft feminine voice on the other end of the line inquired.

"Ummm, yes, yes . . . this is Dr. Profeta over at St. Vincent ER, and I was wondering . . . ummm . . . did my aunt . . . Maria Nichols just die?" There was a pause on the other end of the line. I already knew the answer.

"Dr. Profeta . . . yes, she did, literally, just now . . . she just died. How . . . how did you know?" the female voice nervously cracked.

"I just knew. Thank you for taking such good care of her," I responded as I hung up the phone, my hands trembling.

Aunt Maria, as I always called her, was not actually my aunt. She was my godmother, a Greek Orthodox woman who taught history and Latin at one of the local junior high schools. I was fortunate that she befriended my mother in her early twenties, and in all practical sense became the mother and role model that she never had while growing up. I have no doubt that my mom became a much better parent and person because of her friendship with Maria.

Her legacy to this day continues through every person she ever met. Into their adult lives, her students always visited, called, and loved her. She never referred to them as her pupils as such. They were always: my son, my daughter, or my child. She was worldly and wise beyond her years and was fondly known for her colorful foul language, even in class. When a student would gasp or snicker sideways to her flowery verbiage, she would respond, "If you don't understand that word, I'll be happy to write it on the board and explain it to you in great detail." She never had to oblige them. She taught into her late seventies and was actually grading papers in the hospice prior to her death. She rolled with the punches and laughed at everything.

I recall eating lunch at her house when I was about ten years old. I noticed a little dried food had adhered to my fork. She saw me examining the dirt and gently asked for the fork. She proceeded to wipe it under her arm and give it back to me. "There . . . it's clean now," she said. That may have been my first lesson on how not to 'sweat' the little stuff.

Most fascinating was observing the perspectives of others in regard to her ethnicity and religious background. She kept it a secret from her students. With her olive-colored skin, grey-black hair, and ethnic disposition, she was part every-student. The Jews knew she had to be Jewish; African-Americans were convinced she was a woman of color; Hispanics, Arab Americans, and even Midwest Protestants claimed her as their own. She could speak many languages including French, Italian, Greek, and Yiddish. She would color her dialogue with Japanese, Chinese, Arabic, and Spanish words, whatever it took to connect. No student really knew her ethnicity, and when they inquired, she would reply, "I am all of you." She was literally a human UN unto herself.

As a practicing ER physician, I would occasionally stop by her school, go to her class, and sit and watch her teach and interact with her students. I loved it. It was like watching Michael Jordan or Barry Bonds at work. In our tough public school, with all of its social and economic pressure, she was held in profound reverence by her students and the other teachers. They knew she absolutely loved them, and they loved her.

Nothing fazed Maria. Life on this earth was a wonderful privilege no matter what came her way. She never missed school even while undergoing chemotherapy. A lymph node dissection and mastectomy left her with a chronically swollen arm to match her swollen heart. She went to school bald and sick, but she never gave up. Maria knew that every minute that she spent in the classroom was one more chance to make a difference, to touch a life, to shape a child. The classroom was her home, the desk was her kitchen table, the chalkboard her welcoming hearth. She saw the good in everyone and everything, even in those who had wronged her in life. She was profoundly spiritual and thanked God every day for the blessings she had been given: She defined forgiveness, and it was that quality and my lack of it that seemed to trigger the events that transpired in the ER the night of Maria's death.

Now, let me preface this story by telling you that it is absolutely true (except for changing some names). I make this claim because it is so coincidental and bizarre that even I have trouble believing it sometimes. These events were, however, one of the pinnacle moments in my life when I knew that God was real, and that perhaps I just needed to open my mind and my heart to him more often. It was the day I finally learned to forgive, forget, and move on with my life. It was the day I learned that letting go of hatred is liberating and godly in its simplicity. It was the day that I learned how to laugh at myself. Because in the wee hours of the night of Maria's death, she showed up and taught me a final lesson I will never forget.

After I confirmed the news of her death, I went into my office adjacent to the ER and sat there with my head in my hands, with tears welling up in my eyes as I grieved the loss of my beloved Maria. My mind wandered filled with memories of her, of

Mediterranean pastries, basset hounds, black coffee, long hugs held tightly against large matronly breasts. Then, it happened. An image of Kris Reich intruded on my reflections of this glorious woman.

Now that you know how wonderful my memories of Maria were, multiply that by a negative one thousand, and you get a glimpse of my memories of Kris Reich. This kid was evil incarnate. Growing up as the only Jew on the east side of Indianapolis, he made my childhood a living hell. His last name was Reich to boot—go figure. He was probably about four or five years older than I, and I hadn't wasted any mental energy on him for at least ten years. Truly, this angry and disturbed kid had not entered my mind at any time in the past decade. But now, only moments after Maria's death, all I could think about was the absolute hatred I had for him, a hatred bordering on homicidal rage.

When I tell you that this kid tortured and terrorized me as a child, it is a severe understatement. He constantly called me cheap Jew, kike, Christ-killer, and a myriad of synonyms related to the female anatomy. He threw my bike into the fish pond, bloodied my lip, and beat me to a pulp at every chance. He even pulled a knife on me once, and later threatened to have my parents gassed. This was the most emotionally disturbed kid I have ever known. I trembled at the mere thought of him. I know how a victim of parental child abuse must feel. He was always older and much bigger than I, always capable of hurting me. And while I should've been thinking of nothing but my deceased aunt and my love for her, all I could picture was tracking him down and evening the playing field. You see, I was thirty-seven, now six-feet tall and 200 pounds with a black belt in karate, and was capable of bench-pressing a small village. In addition, I had the resources to track this son of a bitch down. But I didn't have to because thirty minutes later he came to me.

The soft rapping of a fist against the wood door brought me

back to reality. "Medics called, they're bringing in someone in severe respiratory distress," came the nurse's voice from the other side.

"Be right there." I composed myself, wiped the tears from my eyes, blew my nose, took a deep breath, and walked back into the trauma room to await my patient. She was an elderly lady, probably eighty or so. She was slipping out of consciousness in severe respiratory distress from end-stage emphysema or pneumonia; I can't really recall.

I quickly placed an intravenous line in her, sedated the patient, and put her on life support: a breathing tube placed into her lung and a mechanical ventilator to maintain her respirations. She briefly stabilized, but it was clear that with all the other co-morbidities that she would, in most likelihood, die in the next few days. They told me her name and that she was a resident at a local nursing home. From all indications she did not have a signed living will on file. "We need to call a next of kin and get someone in here," I indicated to one of the nurses.

"Here we go," said Gaynell, the nurse in charge. "The next of kin is a sister . . . a Mrs. Reich."

My heart stopped. "Do they have an address for her on Wittier Lane?" I asked.

"Yeah . . . that's it. Do you know them? Are they F.O.P.s?" (F.O.P. is an acronym the nurses jokingly used to describe a 'Friend of Profeta'.)

"Yeah, I know them. And no, they're not F.O.P.s. Would you call Mrs. Reich and fill her in on her sister, and tell her she probably needs to come in." I paused, and for some reason added, "She'll tell you she needs to call her son to bring her in." The nurse just looked at me, appearing to be even more confused. She flipped through the paperwork until she found the phone number and called Mrs. Reich. I returned to my office.

"Dr. Profeta?" Gaynell stuck her head inside the cracked office door. "I reached Mrs. Reich and she is on her way in. And she said she had to call her son to give her a ride. Now what is going on here . . . what don't we know?" she asked tersely, hands on her hip.

I sat with the nurses and told them the story of Maria dying, of me sitting in the office in a stream of consciousness, of the terror that was Kris Reich . . . everything I was feeling. They sat transfixed, kind of freaked out, and completely aware that I was visibly shaking, scared to hell of this man coming to the ER. That made them uneasy. They nervously tried to joke about it. Should security be called, and get leather restraints ready for me, or perhaps sedate me prior to my family encounter. They wanted to know who to call in if I were to get my ass kicked, considering I was the only doc in the hospital. But most of all, they were fascinated by the guy who at that moment had me shaking with a mixture of anger, sadness, and terror. So I did what any other mature, sensible grown-up man would do in this situation; I cowered in my office until they arrived.

There was a knock on the door. Beverly and Gaynell were there. Both had smiles on their face, fighting back laughter. "Dr. Profeta . . . Mrs. Reich and her son are here," with emphasis on son.

"We got your back, Doc. Don't you worry," said Beverly. They both laughed again.

I walked into the patient's room and re-encountered the spawn of Hitler. Twenty minutes later, he was inviting me to play golf.

I had not seen Kris Reich for nearly 29 years, and now this monster, this giant with horns and fangs, with claws the size of a grizzly's and muscles like a pro wrestler, had morphed into a five-foot-four-inch, 150-pound blue-collared librarian. He wore a small ball cap, was missing a few teeth, and he had spindly arms with a small beer belly to boot. He looked about as threatening as my grandma. The nurses just stood staring, watching the story within the story. "This is not Kris Reich," I said to myself. "No way." The nurses kept averting their eyes to keep from laughing.

"Profeta . . . you're not Louis Profeta?" He looked at me questioning himself.

"Yes, I am. You're Kris, aren't you?" I asked, staring intently at him.

"Man, I haven't seen you in probably 25 years. So, you're a doctor. Wow, that's great."

"Yeah," I said simply.

Then he paused, looked around for a second, and let out an uneasy laugh. "Yeah, we used to mix it up a little when we were kids." He moved his fists around in the air in a boxing caricature. "Though, it looks like you could probably take care of me now."

"You better believe it," I responded, my arms triumphantly folded across my chest.

"Yeah . . . well, I wasn't the best kid in the world back then. I had a lot of problems, got involved with the wrong crowd, you know."

And with that I felt like a complete dickhead. There you have it, an apology 29 years in the making. The next hour or so was spent discussing his aunt, catching up on our families, the old neighborhood, and our lives. He invited me to go golfing with him and thanked me for taking such good care of his aunt. And with that he left the ER.

I have no doubt that this was Aunt Maria's intercession, along with divine providence. I am certain that it was her departing gift to me. It was her way of saying, "Let it go. Don't hold grudges, people change, and life is too short to fill your heart with hatred. Energy spent hating someone is a wasted heartbeat." It used to be that when I thought of Kris Reich I would be filled with pure unadulterated anger. Now, all I can do is smile.

Chapter Ten

"Besides . . . I Ain't No Russian"

I've never really understood racism. Having been raised Jewish, the reality of the Holocaust and religious and ethnic persecution seemed atrocious to me, and as alien as walking on Venus. On the other hand, I love being a member of a small religious minority, a family per se. There is something very warm, friendly, and inviting about being a part of something bigger, but not too much bigger than myself—a home away from home.

When my wife and I moved from Indianapolis to Pittsburgh for my residency, I knew that I was moving to a city with a large Jewish community and expected to be welcomed. I knew the transition would be quite easy. The landscape of mezuzah-clad doorways that lined the community of Squirrel Hill would feel familiar. There was the Katz Deli owned by Koreans, which sold the best lox, a huge bagel store, and kosher groceries and pizzerias. The Jewish Community Center was a seven-iron shot away from my front door, if you played a fade. Orthodox children scurried to school past Pinsker's Bookstore. It just felt right, even to a modern guy like me. Mind you. I grew up in Indianapolis: the pickle-loaf, white bread capital of America.

There is sort of an unspoken language among Jews as I am sure there are with other minority groups: we are all in it together, and share very similar values, pasts, hopes, and aspirations for the future. That being said I can also understand that to others that may be viewed as clannish, isolated, and perhaps even sinister. So, when the specter of anti-Semitism raised its vile head in the ER, I was ready to strike back. I just didn't count on it to be so damn funny.

"I hit a deer," he said, slurring his words.

"You hit a deer?"

"No, I said, 'I hit a deer.'"

"Okay . . . did it hit you back?"

He was about 35 or so, dirty, blond-headed, ragged, and of course, drunk. He was dressed in a filthy T-shirt, jeans, and scuffed work boots. He smelled of sour beer and cheap cigarettes, and peered at me through cloudy, bloodshot eyes. His faced was covered with broken glass; part of his upper lip dangled down from a large tear below his nose. His skin was a sea of road rash and asphalt burns. A myriad of small lacerations and missing divots of skin lined his bare tattooed arms, decorated with a slew of swastikas and satanic symbols.

"Do you think it's funny?" he snapped back, his eyes boring into me.

"Yeah, actually, I guess I do," I replied. He let out a stifled grunt trying to keep from laughing, staying in his tough-guy role. I continued my physical exam, looking over all his injuries, making sure that nothing more serious was occurring, like brain or spine trauma, a ruptured spleen or a cracked liver. In the end, I was left only with miles of road rash to clean, glass to remove, lacerations to sew, and one 'five-pack' of beer to drink.

During our encounter, I felt slightly uneasy and perhaps a little threatened by his hostility. After all, he was somewhat physically imposing, not to mention being wild-eyed and drunk. It was evident that this guy lived on the fringe of society, in that dark world of methamphetamines, acid rock, and racism. He said very little and stared through me as I did my exam. I focused my attention on one large laceration in particular on his forearm. It was the size of a silver dollar and coursed around the top of his wrist, elevating one half of a quarter-sized swastika as is burrowed into the fatty layers of skin.

"You ain't one of them foreign doctors, is yah?" he inquired in a thick drawl after a while.

"No," I said, probing around the laceration with a pair of

tweezers. "But I am Jewish, and I find these swastika tattoos very offensive," I responded as I looked up from my work and stared him down. He dropped his eyes for a second and cleared his throat.

"Uhhhh, doc, that don't mean nothing but goddamn independence . . . besides . . . I ain't no Russian." I coughed to keep from exploding with laughter. "Hell. It don't make no difference. You can cut that motherfucker out if you want to," he said, pointing to the large laceration.

"No problem," I said. So, with a little extra lidocaine and creative excision work, I did my part to rid the world of a small piece of racism. I folded the flap of skin in a patch of gauze, and, with a satisfactory smile, dropped it in the trash, closing the lid with a satisfying clap.

I remember thinking briefly as I worked on him that this guy was so dumb he wasn't even a good racist. But then I felt a bit ashamed of myself, that I had prejudged him based on his hard appearance, his low-life persona. I think this guy hit the nail right on the head. His swastika was not about racism; it was about belonging. We all need to feel that we are part of something bigger, an extended family. If we are not so fortunate to have grown up in that environment, we seek it out anywhere we can find it. For many, it is church or religion; for others, it is the military; and for some misguided individuals it is a shadow-world alliance, but one that still serves the basic need of belonging, no matter how perverse its venue.

Later that week, barely sober but pleasant, he returned to have his sutures removed and to bring me a present: dangling from an empty plastic ring was a five-pack of Blatz beer. To this day it was the best beer I have ever tasted.

Chapter Eleven

Louis, Pick Up the Phone...It's God

If you knew my sister Marni when she was a student in high school and college, and then met her ten years later, you would not recognize the woman by her outward appearance, though she would tell you that she is the same person. Marni now lives in a foreign world of Orthodox Judaism, comfortable in a provincial lifestyle of long skirts, modest dress, family, and prayer. She went from being a flamboyant officer in her college sorority, one of the most popular and best-looking girls on campus, to a modest, Conservative Orthodox Jew married with four children on the north side of Chicago. She is devoutly religious and spiritual, somehow making a profound leap from the secular world of a go-to-temple-on-the-holidays Jew, to the steadfast observant world of kosher foods, daily prayer, and strict adherence to the ancient doctrines of Torah and Talmudic study. If you were to ask my sister what led her to pursue this pathway, she would tell you, for lack of a better metaphor, that she was always a 'closet' Orthodox Jew. She always knew she was deeply religious with an unwavering belief in God and committed to the traditional ideals of Judaism. Marni understood this from an early age, but did not feel comfortable practicing it until she was an adult and the commander of her own destiny.

You could always tell, from her youngest of years, that Marni made choices in life with a deep appreciation of how her actions or words would honor or disappoint a higher authority, that being God. She had a special relationship with our grandmother, who lived with us in a garage converted to an apartment. She was a woman who was 'straight off the boat'; after living in the United States for some seventy-five years, she still spoke English like she stepped ashore at Ellis Island yesterday.

Widowed at a young age, our grandma, or Nona as we called her, lit the Shabbat candles every Friday night, kept a kosher kitchen, and started most sentences with a Jewish version of a Ladino 'a dio', or 'dear God' to the rest of us. During Midwest thunderstorms, she could be found huddled on our stairwell, frightened by the sounds that took her back to childhood, to a time when war raged in Salonika. At such times, Marni could be found huddled with her. Before she died, she made me promise her one thing: The photos of her three sons that adorned her TV set would never be separated, even if my dad and one of his brothers had not spoken for some thirty years.

It was this brother-on-brother imposed exile that set the standard for us as children and young adults. It, in essence, gave us permission to hold onto anger for months and even years, pontificating on how we were right and the other person was wrong. For whatever reason, Marni and I fell into some stupid conflict about six months prior to her marriage. I can't recall exactly what the fight was about, but I am absolutely sure I was right and she was wrong, or it may have been the other way around, probably the latter. Anyway, we did not talk or want to have anything to do with each other after that. In fact, I don't even think I sent her a wedding gift. So when I got the call at the ER that a drunk driver had killed her father-in-law, who at the time lived in South Africa, I was hit with a deep sense of sadness that greatly overshadowed my foolish animosity toward her and her husband. I was overwhelmed with loss, and also a feeling of profound guilt that I was not there for her.

I immediately called her and told her how sorry I was. The anguish in her voice was palpable, and it only served to remind me how much I cared for her, and how fragile life is. Marni and her husband readily accepted my offer of airline tickets to fly to Johannesburg to be with his family. After all, I had never bought her a wedding gift. So it was partly guilt money. Maybe it was also divine providence: God's plan to further my understanding of myself, by giving me an opportunity to come to the need of someone other than strangers in the ER, my family in fact.

Interestingly enough, when I called Marni to inquire about some of the issues dealing with the timeline of the story, Marni reminded me that we had not spoken for nearly two years, prior to getting back from the funeral. If you had asked me, I would have said maybe six months at most. It highlighted how sensitive Marni was to this event, and how removed I was or caught up in my own world.

I really have no recollection as to what our fight was about in the first place. Marni, however, knows the issue, but will not remind me. Well, I'm not sure I want to know anyway. What is more amazing and perhaps more providential is that Marni tells me that just one week prior to this devastating event, I sent her an e-mail apologizing to her, reminding her that I wanted her and her husband in my life and in my children's life, essentially washing the slate clean. Amazingly enough, I don't recall sending that email. It was as if God stopped me for a second and said, "Louis, fix things with your sister, make her smile, put her at ease, because I'm about to send her and her husband a doozy." So for nearly two years, that's 104 weeks, we had no real contact until that one week prior to perhaps the worst day of her life. At that moment I listened to God, not with my ears but with my heart.

So often in the ER we meet families that are at odds: separated parents bringing in children with false claims of abuse and neglect to support some custodial claim, children fighting over the wishes of their dying parents, spouses fighting spouses, sister battling a brother, and on and on. For the most part I could care less about what led to their conflict; I just try to remind them about how brief our lives are here on earth. For separated parents, fighting over the welfare of a child, I remind both of them how much more they have in common, their children, than their differences. I am so astounded how people, who could profess their love for each other until the end of time, could with the passage of time come to hate each other, wanting nothing but the worst for the father or mother of their child. They are so consumed by their anger, by petty disputes and affronts, that they lose sight of the heaven around them: glorious sunsets and sunrises, a child's simple smiles, and the soft touch of hands reaching out for comfort that makes life so beautiful.

My relationship with my sister has never been better. Though she, unknowingly, makes me feel slightly guilty for eating shellfish, or driving on the Sabbath. I suppose it's a fair exchange for my numerous off-color 'sham-religious' inquiries like whether oral sex is kosher.

So while it came to a surprise for many in the family that Marni made the transition back to the more formal and traditional style of Judaism, it also made complete sense to me. Knowing the relationship Marni had with our Nona: the years she spent cuddled on her bed, holding her hand, and helping her in her old age, and knowing what a beautiful mother, wife, and friend she has become, it is obvious that like me she was not running from something she feared but instead running to something she truly desired: a higher level of understanding of herself, and a personal relationship with God.

Chapter Twelve

A Peek Under the Makeup

It sickens me to see 'child' and 'abuse' together in the same sentence. I was always on the lookout for its telltale signs in children, especially on late-night visits to the ER, but it never really had much of a visceral impact on me until I had children of my own.

When Damien came to the ER, this small, angelic child was a battered mosaic of blues, purples, and dark green bruises against a pale ebony canvas. I tried in vain to bring this poor child back to life, but the massive brain and liver trauma, brought about by being slammed to the floor for crying, was more than his two-year-old frame could sustain. As expected the culprit was the boyfriend of the teenage mother, who was unprepared to care for any child, let alone one that was not his own, taking out his hidden, real, or imaginary life frustrations on the easiest target at hand.

I was asked to testify at the mother's trial on neglect charges. She claimed to have not noticed all the bruising coating the corpse of Damien—bruises that reflected a pattern of repetitive trauma. The prosecutors came to my home, a manila folder in hand stuffed with autopsy photos of a bloody scalp peeled back to reveal the fleshy undersurface now covering the child's face, which exposed the deep linear skull trauma that contributed to his death—his murder.

The day he died in the ER was one of the worst days of my career. I could have dealt with the accidental nature of his death but not with the intentional sadistic abuse and neglect at the hands of this now-incarcerated animal; he pled guilty and was sentenced to more than fifty years in prison. I came home late in the evening, numb and confused. How could God allow something like this to happen? A question that I am certain many ask about the Holocaust, or even natural disasters like Hurricane Katrina for that matter.

I walked to my eldest child's bedroom door and looked in on him fast asleep, not a care in the world, and I started to cry. I quietly climbed into his bed, stroked his soft brown hair, and holding him close while taking in the sweet smell of talc and baby shampoo, my lips pressed against his small cheek. Though he never awoke that night, I promised Max to love him with every heartbeat God grants me and with every breath God provides. I also made a promise to say the Jewish prayer for the dead for Damien every day for a year. I am sure I missed some days, but I tried. Part of me figured that, if his parents did not truly love him enough to keep him safe in life, at least I could do my part in death. I think part of me also wanted to tell God, "I'm different from the man who killed this child. Do you hear me God? He is not me and will never be me."

What is it that leads someone to abuse and torture the frailest of us all, those most in need of our protection, whether it is a child, the elderly, or the infirmed? What is the root problem? Is it simply anger management, is it being able to dominate someone or something when you have no control over your own world, or is it simply being sadistic? While physical abuse is certainly active in nature with mom or dad beating the child, even more pervasive is passive child abuse; this is even more frustrating since it is completely sanctioned.

I would include the parent that rarely bathes their child, leaving him or her caked in dirt, head filled with lice and fungus, essentially setting the stage for a lifetime of self-neglect and lack of self-respect. I would include the parent whose clothes are so filled with cigarette smoke that even breathing for the physician is a chore, let alone the effects the residual smoke has on the small delicate eardrums, lung cells, eyes, and health of their child. I would include the separated parents that come to the ER fighting each other, spending more time assigning blame than caring for their child. I would include the parents who have money for cigarettes and alcohol but not for Tylenol, tooth-brushes, bars of soap, shampoo, booster seats, diaper rash ointment, and bus or cab fare to their pediatrician's office.

While most in the healthcare industry like to call this neglect, or situational stressors, or whatever politically correct nomen-clature comes to mind, I would prefer to call it what it really is: abuse. Any time you are put in charge of the welfare of another, especially your own child, and you do not maximize all the resources available to you to ensure that your small bundle of life is safe, clean, fed, and educated, then you are abusing that gift you have been given. It is an abuse of God's gift of life. As a parent the child owes us nothing. We owe them everything. We can only hope that by committing all our effort, love, energy, and resources to their well-being, we will raise a child who will grow to honor us—principally by doing the same for their own children. It is in all sense a self-fulfilling prophecy.

There is a bizarre illness called Munchausen's disease by proxy. I have seen this problem on numerous occasions. It is a confusing psychological condition in which the parent, typically the mother in more than 90 percent of the cases, actually fakes illness or symptoms in their own child. One school of thought claims that it is an attention-getting mechanism on the part of the parent. What is terrifying is that the case fatality ratio is greater than many forms of childhood cancer. That means that a child of a parent suffering from this condition has a better chance of dying under their care than if they contracted certain types of lymphoma or other cancers. Can you imagine any physician or healthcare provider ignoring this prospect?

Many years ago I cared for a little five-year-old boy; his mother brought the child to the ER frantic that he had a fever of 105 and suffered a febrile seizure just thirty minutes prior to their arrival. The child in question was sitting on the bed, laughing, playing with a rubber glove with no signs of any illness, and with no fever. I listened to his mother's story with a great degree of skepticism, at first figuring that she had been confused. Perhaps, I rationalized, mom thought the child felt warm, and then he had some activity that may have looked like a seizure. It sounded feasible; that is until I requested and reviewed all the old records from our hospital and the nearby pediatric referral hospital. What I found was both chilling and distressing.

By age five this small boy had had multiple spinal taps, numerous CT scans, EEGs, MRIs, blood draws, and IV lines too numerous to count. The results were that no one had ever found a single, real concrete illness—each diagnosis started with "probable" or "possible" or "can't rule out". That's medical jargon for 'beats the hell out of me what's going on; let's dish it off to another consultant'. Yet the tests went on and on, the chart getting thicker, taking on an authority all of its own, as if to say, "He must be sick . . . look at the size of the chart." In fact, in five years this child had not gone more than a week without showing up in some ER, Med-check, or physician's office, undergoing hundreds of inpatient and outpatient tests all with the goal of 'making the correct diagnosis'. That's when I said—and admittedly with trepidation—"Enough." I walked into the room, looked right at the mom, and told her I thought she was lying . . . not mistaken . . . but outright lying. Needless to say she was incensed, yelled about suing me and taking my license and so on, and proceeded to leave until security stopped her at the door. Of course, I had alerted the officers in advance. I notified the mother that I was calling child welfare and taking immediate custody of her child on charges of abuse by Munchausen's disease by proxy. The child was placed in foster care for six months, during which he never so much as had a runny nose, cough, or fever, let alone a seizure. Mom was forced by the courts to get psychological counseling and, as is the case with nearly all Munchausen's patients, once confronted with the facts, the abuse stopped and they were reunited in a healthy mother-and-child atmosphere.

Upon review of this case, what was most disturbing was how often the prospect of Munchausen's disease was mentioned in consult notes. Every doctor wanted every other doctor to take the reins, stick their neck out, but not them. In every sense, we as physicians were as guilty of abuse as his mother. Nobody ever forced our hands to insert needles, administer medications, order tests, and contribute to the problem. We were given the gun, the mechanism of abuse, and instead of putting a lock on it, we pulled the trigger for five years over and over again.

Over the years I have been invited to give a fair number of lectures to educators on identifying abuse and teaching basic childhood safety. So often I am met with questions that focus more attention on the legalities of getting it wrong than getting it right. It seems no one wants to get involved anymore. What is it that has led us to turn our backs so many times to injustice?

I always reaffirm to these educators that I have been wrong on occasion, but more important, the parents of these children are typically more grateful for my concern than they are about being falsely questioned about abuse. In fifteen years I can count on two hands how many times a teacher has brought an abused child to the ER. It is action that happens far too infrequently. In perhaps half of these situations, the child has not been abused. Usually, it is the misidentification of Mongolian spots on the rump of a child (a large bluish pigmented patch that looks like a huge bruise). In each case the parents laughed it off and told the teacher it was no big deal. In most of the other cases, the abuse that initiated the investigation paled in comparison to what lay below the surface.

Most recently a teacher brought a child to the ER because she noticed a small bruise on the young boy's forehead that was partly covered with makeup in a pathetic attempt to hide it. When I exposed the child fully, wiped off all the makeup, the child had literally a hundred marks ranging from belt loops, handprints, bites, and bruises in various stages of healing. This teacher saved this child's life. Nothing in her career will have a greater impact than the simple act of her getting involved that day, not closing her eyes, and standing up and demanding an explanation.

We not only owe it to the weak and the disenfranchised to get involved, but we owe it to our own children. We owe our involvement to the Damiens of the world who were slammed to the ground for crying and to the six million Jews who died while millions more turned their backs because they did not, for whatever reason, want to get involved. There is an ancient Talmudic saying: "To have saved a life is to have saved the whole world." We owe it to God and the world to keep our eyes open, to make a stand for those who can't stand up for themselves, to take a moment, however brief, and to look under the makeup.

Chapter Thirteen

One Man's Hero, Another Man's Bum

As I've often said, I am a son of a bitch at times. I can't help it. Well, maybe I could if I really tried. It's just that I get tired of trying to be everything to everybody. I think it would be easier if I ran a bait shop or worked in a bookstore. Let's face it, most people who come to the bait shop aren't ill, tired of waiting, or in a bad mood. They're just going fishing.

When my neighbor Dave invited me to go to the Cayman Islands with him for five days of scuba diving and relaxation at his condo, I couldn't decline. My wife, understanding my need to clear my head, thought it would be great for me to get away. I had entered one of those down periods where I needed to be rebooted. But I warned Dave, "One of the problems traveling with an ER doctor is that something always happens. I'll most certainly have to perform some type of medical intervention, or someone strikes up a conversation and I'll end up giving advice on prostate testing or menstrual irregularities." In fact we bet $50 on it, but I had to promise not to seek it out—it just had to happen. Well, it did and with a vengeance.

We had just arrived at the Detroit Airport and disembarked to catch our plane to the Caribbean. The minute I stepped out of the walkway, I noticed a mild commotion against the far wall. I could make out the typical orange color of emergency equipment and oxygen tanks alongside one of those small airport golf carts. A security guard was fumbling with the O2 canister; a few people were kneeling. An African-American family milled around the perimeter talking to airport personnel. No one seemed too concerned at the time. Dave nudged me away from viewing the scene, saying, "Let's go get a drink, we've got time."

"Sure," I said, and we walked a little farther into the concourse, my head still slightly tilted in the direction of the crowd. "Doesn't look too bad anyway, someone probably just fell or fainted?" I took a few more steps but then slowed down.

Dave shrugged his shoulders and glanced at me. "You want to go check it out?" I paused for a second, rocked in my stance, trying to pull myself toward the airport bar. The Heineken sign beckoned.

"Yeeaaahhh, I should just take a peek, make sure nothing really bad is going on." We slowly ambled over to the gathering in no particular hurry.

By that time someone had put an oxygen mask, though not attached to the tank, onto the young man lying on the floor. His eyes were open and he was breathing. He was a big African-American teenager, probably 260 pounds, six feet tall. He was dressed in big baggy pants and a Pistons team jacket, and he was lying sprawled out in a pile of winter apparel.

Quietly, I approached the guard, or ticket agent, I can't recall. "I'm Dr. Profeta, an ER doc. Anything I can do, or do you need some help?"

I've learned over the years that if you charge in with a puffed-out chest like Underdog, you come across as a prick, especially to those who have already stopped to render assistance. Good Samaritans, for the most part, do a great job in often demanding situations. They are honorable people using the skills they have to make a difference. They are just trying to help, and that takes courage in every sense of the word. To most ER docs, stopping to help is a rewarding, simple chore, like doing the laundry. Besides, there is nothing like folding warm towels.

After a very brief survey and introduction all around, I came to the quick realization that this kid was f%#$d. Sweat was pouring off this man-child; his heart rate was like forty. He barely had a pulse, and to top it off, on the side of his scalp was a huge elliptical scar still scabbed over from where he had had a bullet removed from his brain a few weeks earlier. But that was nothing compared to his breathing which sounded like he was sucking air though a coffee stirrer. That was when I noticed that someone had cut a breathing hole in this kid's neck during his hospital stay. He must have been on life support for a while and had to have a tracheotomy that recently had been sewn. His grandparents were fairly uninformed, only aware that he had just been discharged from a rehab center, and had become short of breath in the airport.

So now all I could think was, "Is this kid is going to die?" He most certainly had scar tissue narrowing his airway from his neck surgery. There was no way I was going to be able to force enough air into his lungs via mouth to mouth, and I was not about to thrust a knife blade through this kid's throat in the middle of the Detroit Airport. Though honestly, I thought it would have been pretty cool to do and I would have done it if necessary. I even tried to force the neck incision open with my bare hands and tried to get my finger into his airway, but the skin wouldn't budge. Thank God that the paramedics arrived.

I immediately moved to the side, informing them I was an ER doctor, and I filled them in on the situation. I offered my expertise and told them I would be willing to talk to their online medical command physician. That was my way of making the medics aware that I really knew what I was talking about. It let them know that I understood that they were in charge, and that I have all the respect in the world for them as healthcare providers. After all, I was on my way to the airport bar; this was their job. Subsequent after sizing me up, they were more than happy to let me take control of this complex case. That is the sign of a great medical team: no egos, just patient care, and doing what is right.

When medical students are co-managing a very sick patient with me at the bedside, I can often see how nervous and apprehensive they become, especially around someone who is unstable. I repeat a standard phrase to them that always seems to remove some of the tension: "Don't be afraid or nervous until I am. But when I am, be damn afraid." This was one of those cases where I had to admit that I was damn afraid, although I didn't say anything.

The medics were trying to bag ventilate this kid, but we could barely squeeze air into his lungs. His teeth were clenched tightly together and we could not pry open his mouth. By that time, the young man was covered in vomit, and getting an IV line in his arms, hands, or external jugular veins in his neck was impossible due to his obesity and lack of visible veins from his recent hospitalization. His pulse rate was slowing, and it was obvious he was going to go into full cardiac arrest soon.

"Give me a big IV needle; what sedative or paralysis drugs do you guys carry?" I asked urgently. My commanding voice was strained even to me.

"Valium. That's all we have for sedation . . . oh, and some morphine." I grabbed the needle and felt hard for the carotid artery. I remember silently asking God for help to get a line into this kid. I felt the pulse angled to the side and drove the needle deep into his neck, hoping to hit the external jugular vein. Dark, rich, and heavenly venous blood percolated up through the top of the catheter. Now I know how Moses felt when he hit that rock. The medic immediately slammed in a boatload of Valium and morphine. This loosened the kid's mandible and lungs, briefly making it a little easier to bag ventilate him. I grabbed an intubation blade (sort of like a large spatula with a light), lay back on the floor, and pulled this giant onto my chest. Using the blade while the medic carefully got the vocal cords in view, I pushed aside a mass of huge tongue, scar tissue, and vomit seasoned with 'Beef-A-Roni' to snake a small tube directly into his lungs, one that I would normally have used on a child. Instantly the tube fogged with heavenly condensation as trapped air from his over-inflated chest escaped from his stressed lungs. His heart rate quickly improved, his blood pressure returned, and he survived, much to everyone's relief.

After we got him on a gurney, we all remained quiet for a second; I followed the medics out into the ambulance where we secured all the lines, spoke with the receiving hospital, and wrote up the run sheet. I talked with the medics, and we all agreed that this was the single hardest airway lifesaving rescue we had ever taken part in. We exchanged pats on the back, and some brief guy hugs, and parted ways, all of us feeling like heroes. That is, until Dave and I hit the Cayman Islands with me $50 richer.

We had about ten minutes to get to our plane. But Northwest Airlines had called the pilot to hold departure for us heroes. They gave us some drink coupons, and two hours and forty minutes later, I was standing on a beach in the Cayman Islands: the power of travel. Needless to say, the adrenalin surge I was experiencing on the plane was excessive. I knocked down a couple of Tanqueray and tonics with extra lime, listened to music, and rehashed the near catastrophe over and over with Dave, who just shook his head for two hours and sarcastically laughed, "Only you, Profeta. This could happen only to you."

Dave has no medical background and is about 15 years older than I and a new grandpa. He sells novelty lighters, convenient store items, gag gifts; actually, some of it is pretty cool stuff. My kids love going to his office. They come home with naked cherub key chains that pee—all of those crazy items you see at the gas station. It's good to have a friend like Dave, who sells pooping pig key chains; it keeps things in perspective.

We made it to the condo, where Dave plopped down on the couch. "You need to go for a walk and cool down; you're wired for sound," he told me.

It didn't take much for me to realize that I was experiencing a touch of posttraumatic epinephrine overdrive. This comes when the last drop of adrenaline has been forced into your bloodstream by those damn adrenal glands, which are the lifeblood of ER doctors, battlefield soldiers, and Robin Williams doing standup comedy.

"I'm gone, enough said," I replied as I donned a swimsuit, grabbed a towel and a bottle of water, and headed down the pearly white sands of Seven Mile Beach. Riding high, I was unaware that my world would soon be turned upside down by, of all things, a cheap plastic chair.

I walked about a quarter of a mile down the beach, which was surprisingly deserted. It was, after all, the middle of the week during the off-season. I meandered past a couple of luxury hotels and other condo complexes. I strolled beneath the palms, letting the sound of the waves and the salt air wash away visions of vomit, bullet wounds, and near death from my strained psyche.

I came upon a cluster of about forty beach chairs strewn around in front of an older complex, all for the most part tossed haphazardly. I sat on one of these cheap dime-store chairs, gently sinking my toes into the soft powdery sand. I closed my eyes, relishing the pure unspoiled splendor of the moment. And for me, at that instant in time, I had found it . . . my Shangri-la, my center. That is, until this rotten, pissant, skinny, little son of a bitch burst into my world.

"Excuse me . . . do you live here?"

I squinted at the sickly thin silhouette of an older man framed against the Caribbean blue. His wrinkled, overexposed, tanned hide was partially hidden by a baggy Speedo as he stood with his shaded face between me and the subtle bobbing of sailboats in the shallows.

"I'm sorry . . . what?"

"Do you live here? If you don't live here, you can't sit in these chairs," he said defiantly. "We have lots of problems with cruise ship people taking these chairs. So you can't sit here."

I had to admit at first I thought it was a joke; perhaps, it was Dave setting me up, or some Cayman candid camera. I laughed and looked around. "I mean it," he stammered, "get the fuck out of here. You didn't even put a towel down. No one wants your sweat on their chair."

I sat stone still. It was no joke, and in a few seconds I was about to do something I would surely regret. Mister this-is-my-chair-and-you-are-a-piece-of-shit had just lit the wrong fuse at the wrong time, and I was going to end the day by beating this old man senseless on the beach in front of his condo. I even looked around to see if anyone was watching us. Could I get away with it? Where would I hide the body? Do sharks feed in the shallows? What is the rate of decomposition of a male corpse in full Caribbean sun? Still, I was able to maintain a sense of self-control and just stared blankly at him.

"I am just sitting here," I said slowly, enunciating each word with the precision of a fine Swiss watchmaker.

"No, you're not," he yelled, spittle flying from his tobacco-stained mouth. Just then this wisp of a man reached down, grabbed the legs of the chair, and dumped me head-first into the sand. I jumped to my feet in a rage. And then it hit me. With my quick ER physician reflexes and keen sense of observation, I quickly noticed the man's breath had a harsh odor of tobacco and early-morning scotch; he was wearing a T-shirt with the name of a drug company known for hypertensive medication. A hypertensive, type-A personality, early coronary disease, high lung-cancer risk, smoking drinker, I thought.

"Oh my," I said softly, almost angelically; the voice of a revered saint was calling from my soul. I gazed at him with no malice or ill-will, just pure understanding. "You don't know, do you?"

He was instantly confused, looking at me perplexed. "What?"

I reached and softly grabbed his hand, putting a hand on his shoulder, and leaned into him. "You have six months. It's lung cancer, aggravated by your hypertension and early coronary artery disease. The alcohol is also taking its toll; you don't know it's there . . . but it's there. You have six months left to live. I'm so sorry."

He staggered back, fear racing across his burnt face. I held my gaze tighter, my eyes never leaving his.

"Six months," I repeated. "You should make plans." And with that I picked up my towel, righted the chair, and walked away, leaving the cowering shell of a man rushing to get away from me.

Before you think that I had some psychic premonition, some heavenly sixth sense of foreshadowing, let me set the record straight. I have no idea if 'Mr. Chair' had lung cancer. And let's be honest, if the tumor had been sticking a foot out of his chest at that instant, I doubt I would have given a damn. But I'll bet on one thing for sure; he got a chest X-ray and a complete workup that week. And I bet he spent the next six months looking over his shoulder. I like to imagine that perhaps I stopped his world and he was a changed man, and saw the error of his ways. I tested this theory.

Two days later Dave and I were walking back from one of the hotels when I caught sight of the man near where our first encounter took place. Dave, who thought the story was a hoot, clenched his teeth to keep from laughing, trying to keep me from straying from my path. The man was huddled near a palm tree, trying to hide from view. I looked straight ahead, pretending not to notice, until I was parallel to him. Then I stopped. Slowly, mechanically, I turned and stared right at him. I lifted six fingers, as he fled into the condo complex.

Well, if this story makes you take me off your Christmas or Hanukkah list, so what. Some people do need to be put in their place or reminded of their humanity, and as I said before, I can be a son of a bitch at times. Occasionally, we all have trouble sorting out the heroes from the bums, or in my case is it the other way around?

Chapter Fourteen

The Crackhead, the Grifter, and the Pinstriped Felon

As bad as it sounds, some people just never die, as much as they want to end it. Every ER in America has them: the crackhead, the grifter, and the pinstriped felon. They are the walking dead, those who live just a few inches above the dirt, constantly knocking on heaven's door, or more often pounding on the gates of hell with a ferocity few of us can comprehend. Some have everything, and others have absolutely nothing. Some may at first glance seem beautiful, full-breasted with supple lips and soft skin. Some are even finely pressed versions of model citizens clad in pinstriped suits. Still others are dirty in soiled undergarments and wet socks, frosted with renal failure and crack cocaine. All of them want to die, but never pull the trigger. And, unlike those with depression, they never admit having a death-wish to themselves or others. On some level they seem mad at the world, adamantly rejecting any help. They actually seem to enjoy your disdain of them. It is what makes them feel alive, connected. They often fuel your animosity, only to weep in self-pity and apologize for their behavior just at the point you are ready to throw them out. You'll forgive them, only to have them assign blame to you for all their ills, and the vicious cycle will start all over again.

They are the moral felons who in many instances never commit a real crime, or have never been caught. They might forge a bad check here, forget to pay a debt there, or lure the spouse of a friend into a lurid sexual affair only to reveal the relationship to all who will listen. You search for adjectives to describe your feelings in regard to their behavior, but nothing seems to fit. Then, it hits home; you just don't trust them. A thousand interactions allow those of us in the ER to pick them out very quickly. We have psychiatric labels for them. They are called sociopaths; they have atypical bipolar disorder, borderline personality disorder, and a host of other psychological complexes.

And while I have never verbalized any of the above in the sanctuary of the ER, I am certain these opinions have been voiced at one time or another, perhaps over the second scotch. I have caught myself almost falling prey to counter-transference (psychological terminology for becoming angry with your patient). But unless your name is Jesus or Job, it is almost impossible to refrain. I have been known to walk into a room to treat such a patient with a medical student, nurse, or resident in tow, shaking my head in disgust. I stop in front of the closed door, look at the student, wipe my hand across my face, and say, "Time to put on my concerned look." And with a flick of my hand, my demeanor will change, and I will shift into my doctor cum actor persona. I tell my students that it is okay if, at times, you don't really care: just try not to act like you don't really care. Providing healthcare is not about how you feel, it's about how the patient feels.

I have a friend, a well-known physician, who never seems to get upset. "On the contrary," he tells me, "I get angry all the time, especially when dealing with hospital executives on finance issues. I am a black belt when it comes to polite, passive-aggressive communication. 'I see' means 'go %&*#@ yourself'. 'That's interesting' means 'you're a moron',' and 'that's really interesting' means 'you're a complete moron'."

I think it's a brilliant way of getting angry without displaying it. It fulfills a great human need to honor your feelings and express your anger, even if the other party is unaware of it. For interactions with your mildly difficult ER patients, these mechanisms work just fine for both parties. But for the grifter, the crackhead, and the pinstriped felon, this is child's play. They are clued in to such behavioral modification since they use it all the time. They have been master manipulators since the day they squirted out of the womb. They are precision athletes, pioneers of deceit. While some are capable of great professional accomplishments, most are practitioners of profound disasters on the interpersonal sphere. Their personal lives are sometimes a sine wave fluctuation from wealth and accomplishment to bankruptcy, addiction, and stress center admissions. They will be your friend and ally one day, and the next day they would just as soon put a bullet in your head, pour arsenic in your tea, or destroy your reputation through lies and innuendos. So as a physician your only real defense is to determine that they don't have a life-threatening problem, avoid contact as much as possible, get Social Services involved quickly, and get them the hell out of your ER, before they have the opportunity to become a tsunami destroying the morale of the entire department.

I usually am able to identify them by a silent whisper that I hear very plainly in my ear: 'careful'. It's the asp in Eden sending out a long hiss of caution: 'careful'. Because whatever they say, what they mean is: "My chief complaint, the problem that brought me here, pales in comparison to the underlying pathology that defines me." But the law is plain: We must, and should, see all comers. We must and should do our best to provide the best possible treatment. We must and should maintain our objectivity and do our best to provide comfort. However, we must never be forced to suffer from physical or emotional abuse or the threat of such. And we must never allow the care of others in the ER to suffer the ranting of a few lunatics. I feel the ER should never give a green light to the worst display of human behavior or let it go unchallenged.

"I want to talk to the nursing supervisor," the voice screams with spittle and vile hatred. "I'll sue you fucking assholes . . . all of you. I'm going to call my lawyer now." You see only a seasoned pro would ask specifically for the nursing supervisor. Others with valid complaints simply inquire about whom they need to talk with to air a concern about patient care, etc.

So you wait for the sine wave to ease back down to a baseline, perhaps take a dip down into the realm of actual civilized behavior by offering a meal tray, the opportunity to smoke, a free cab voucher, some lighthearted discussion, or a few pain pills; then you quickly discharge them to the sanctity of their own personal hell, just to get some respite from their bizarre antisocial behavior. You feel no sense of guilt for those who ultimately refuse to care for their self, their family, or what few friends they have. And they certainly don't care about you.

All you can do is to offer them a chance for change, protect the others in your charge, and like the battlefield medic who must choose by their injury between those you can treat and save and those you can't, you can't restart every dead heart, even the ones that haven't stopped beating yet.

Chapter Fifteen

Harry Carter's Shoes

He was, in all practical purposes, the first patient whom, for a prolonged period of time, I had ever cared for and with whom I had established any real bond, and the first to die under my supervision. He gave me a lesson in contrition and showed me that everyone has a soul, a spirit capable of reflecting God's goodness, one with the potential to impact the lives of others, even if that exchange was just a brief, seven-word sentence. Harry left that mark on me and changed my life forever.

His life must have been very hard. He was beaten and bruised by time and through service to his country, and spent his final few months cooped up in a dark windowless room at the Pittsburgh VA Hospital. He was in my charge for nearly a month. I spent a good deal of time with him because he was sick as hell. Harry was about forty, had a form of bone cancer and hepatitis, and required an untold number of blood transfusions. His years of intravenous drug abuse had ravaged his veins, and he was covered with sores and scars of prior battles. His eyes were yellow with liver failure and contrasted sharply against his dark black skin. He was tall and sinewy, and well over six feet with a head of hair like Don King's. His room had the constant sickening smell of sweat and bloody stool, which tended to keep the nurses from working too hard to provide care, which for that VA, unfortunately, seemed to be the norm rather than the exception. I recall discovering one of my patients there dead and stiff in rigor mortis, a condition that takes time to set.

Harry had low platelets (cells used for clotting blood) and consequently suffered from ongoing rectal bleeding, which for a man of his stature was humiliating, not to mention uncomfortable. He was constantly soiling himself and required a lot of nursing attention. As fast as I could put blood into Harry, it would break down or leak out from some orifice. His final weeks were certainly horrible, but this guy never complained. He always had a smile when I saw him and a new joke every day. He called me "Doc" and always made an effort to tell me what a good job I was doing. Each morning I was met with a "Hello" or a "Good morning, Doc," and he made sure to send me on my way with a heartfelt "See you later" or "Have a good day."

Unfortunately, all our therapies came to no avail. He failed chemotherapy; he was not a candidate for a bone marrow transplant, and all we could do was to keep replacing his blood and platelets. During one restless night, his movements pulled the only workable IV out, and I was forced to put a central line in Harry. This is a very large IV line that you place in one of the major veins leading back to the heart. In his case I was putting it into the subclavian vein, right under his collarbone. This procedure was painful and difficult. He was a big man, though markedly volume depleted and anemic, had numerous prior central lines, and was a mass of scar tissue from prior surgical sites. I spent a long time trying to place the line. He was restless, short of breath from severe anemia, and difficult to keep still. It was a frustrating procedure, and during the course of his movement to get comfortable, I proceeded to stick myself with a contaminated needle.

"Damn it, Harry, you have to hold still. I just stuck myself!" I glared at him, ripping back the sterile drape. I snapped my gloves off and tossed them onto the floor in disgust. Then, I proceeded to squeeze as much blood out of my wound as possible, washing and scrubbing it with Betadine, hoping that this IV drug abuser was not HIV positive. Harry remained quiet, and then I heard it . . . those seven words, the most painful words ever spoken to me.

"I'm sorry, Doc . . . are we still friends?"

I stood stone silent. Here was this guy dying of cancer, a grown man lying in a diaper full of bloody stools, having someone drive a large needle into his neck, lying in bed day after day in a shit-hole of a room, with no friends or visitors, and all he can think about is hurting my feelings—whether or not I was still his friend. I was so ashamed of myself I could not even look at him.

In that instance Harry Carter had shown more class and more compassion than I had shown in my entire life. "Harry," I said, finally looking at him with my hand on his shoulder, "of course we're still friends, and I'm the one who should be sorry. I didn't mean to snap at you . . . I was just frustrated when I couldn't get the line in, knowing you're sick . . . and . . ."

"It's okay, Doc. I'll be still, and you can go ahead and try it again," he interrupted me.

I looked over and smiled; he had more confidence in me than I had in myself at that age. "Okay, Harry. Let's give it another shot." And with that, the line slid in more easily than any I have placed since that day.

But a few weeks later, I had to sit with Harry and explain that he was going to die, and that we just could not give him blood faster than he was losing it. "Okay, I guess that's it," he simply said. "You did all you could do . . . I guess it's time for me to go." Tears welled up in his yellow eyes. I called his next of kin and let them know he would probably die within the next 24 hours.

About five hours later, Harry's respiration rate sped up as blood left his body, and he soon became air-hungry and delirious, and he slipped into a coma. That's when he walked into the room—his son, most likely. He was a tall, robust younger version of Harry, a specter from the mean Hill Street Blues of Pittsburgh. He was dressed in a bulky coat, a ball cap, his collar protectively pulled up, hands tucked in his pockets, sheltering himself from the world. I watched from afar as he pulled up a chair, lowered his head, and held Harry's hand for a short time. Then, he got up, reached down, and picked up Harry's high-top tennis shoes and left the room without saying a word. As I sat with Harry while he died, all I could think about were his tennis shoes and how hard they would be to fill.

Chapter Sixteen

I Went into Medicine for the Money

It's true. I went into medicine for the money. Yes, I know what I said at my interview for medical school.

"So, Mr. Profeta, tell us why you want to attend Indiana University and become a doctor."

"Well, sir, you see, when I was younger, I was involved in a horrible accident...blah, blah, blah...and, well, I saw the way my doctors took care of me...blah, blah, blah...and it had a huge impact on me...blah, blah, blah...and, well, sir, I have always loved science...blah, blah, blah...and I did a lot of soul searching...blah, blah, blah, blah...and that's about it, sir. I really hope to be able to fulfill my calling and become a physician."

Now, if I really had been able to answer the question honestly it would have been something like this: "Well, sir, I have always been insecure and trying to look good in the eyes of others. We never had a lot of money growing up and I was always envious of the kids whose parents had big houses, belonged to country clubs, and got to go to Florida on vacation. I knew I didn't have the stomach for office work so I thought, how could I make a lot of money, get respect, and act like God at the same time? Then it hit me: I'll go into medicine. I mean, let's face it; you have a great gig here. You make good coin, get the best reservations, and even ski trips to Aspen. Well, I want that too. And I'm smart, top ten percent of my class. I mean really, how tough is it?"

Now, if I were interviewing a student, that kid would be at the top of my list; smart, honest, a real go-getter. Fortunately, that is not part of my job description, so I get to leave that to someone else, someone wiser and a heck of a lot better judge of character than me.

I am convinced that medical schools don't really care about our true motives as pre-medical students. They just act like they do. They ask all the right questions and set us up to hear exactly what they want to hear.

"So, Mr. Profeta...who is your hero?"

"Well, sir, that would be my father...blah, blah, blah...worked eighty hours a week pushing a broom...blah, blah, blah...first to graduate...blah, blah, blah." But they know all of our answers are well-rehearsed bull (except that my dad really is my hero, he just doesn't know what a broom is). What they want is to see if we're prepared with our bull; have we anticipated their questions, what quality of verbal vomit can we regurgitate at a moment's notice? Are we quick on our feet, can we handle the pressure, are we driven to succeed, are we a reasonably honest person, is there a home detention bracelet strapped to the ankle, can we speak English? You see, they know something that we as young pre-med students don't know: that saving a life changes you forever.

They know that once a patient holds you in their confidence, thanks you, and relies upon you, they leave a mark. They chip away at your ego, they whittle away at your greed, and they chop down your self-centeredness, leaving you a physician. Medical school is the equivalent of army boot camp; it can take the most dysfunctional high IQ prick and turn them into a person of character. I know, because I was one of them.

If there is one thing that I have learned about doctors it is that we for the most part are honorable people, out trying to do our part to make the world a little better. In most instances we deserve the respect we are given. We truly care for our patients, cry when we make mistakes, and thank God when we and our patients triumph. We spend hours away from our families, answer phones in the middle of the night, and stay late. We miss ball games, Girl Scout meetings, and school plays. We apologize constantly to our family and friends for being absent from weddings, bar-mitzvahs, and milestones in our children's lives, often for people whom we do not even know.

So, we may not all start with the best of motives or the purest of intentions. But, over the course of our careers and our lives we are touched so often by the souls of our patients and by the hands of God that we become what we never expected to be...servants of the almighty and the guardians of compassion and human dignity.

Chapter Seventeen

Uncle Al

The prisoner section of Wishard Hospital is a small window into a world few of us get to see outside of TV crime dramas. It is a medical theater of loud drunken obscenities, desperate addicts, and beat-up street fighters. It is the temporary refuge of sick prisoners and those acting sick to get a respite from prison. It is handcuffs and leather restraints, big security guards, and black polished firearms that match finely shined boots. The clanging of chains grating across bedrails creates a strange wind-chime symphony to accompany the electric tones, door alarms, and pagers. I always thought the medical students in their sharp white coats and innocent faces stood out in stark contrast in this ward, something like a daisy on the battlefield of Gettysburg.

"Profeta," he said abruptly, staring at my name tag. "You related to Al Profeta?" His voice was tense, stern, and accusatory. The other medical students, attending physicians, and residents stood aside, awaiting my response. The man in the four-way leather restraint was strapped to the bed, a lion waiting to get a once-over by the vet.

"Yeah, I am . . . he's my uncle," I said slowly, deliberately, showing not an ounce of fear. Anger welled up inside of me at the thought that this might be one of the sons-a-bitches that shot my Uncle Al. That's when a huge grin broke out over his face, revealing a smile that was missing several front teeth.

"I'm Maurice!" he said jubilantly, with a really big emphasis on the 'Mo'. "I used to be his bag boy; you tell him Maurice said hi . . . you tell him, you hear? I love yoh uncle; he's a good man . . . now don't you forget . . . that's Maurice," again he emphasized the 'Mo'. I patted him on his strapped-down arm and laughed.

"No problem, Mo. I'll tell him." I walked away smiling.

"A friend of the family?" asked my attending physician. All the other residents and students laughed as we walked down the hall to finish our rounds.

Uncle Al, my dad's older brother by fifteen years, is a proud member of Tom Brokaw's 'Greatest Generation'. A few years back, in the corner booth of a Bob Evans, I talked with Uncle Al about his war years, something he had never really done before. He seemed ready and perhaps relieved. Like other young men of the 1940s, he entered the army to save the world from Fascism. Assigned to the 97th Division, he was shipped overseas to serve as a replacement for infantry in the 5307. In time he found himself in Camp Rangar in northern India, and he was later sent to fight the Japanese along the Burma Road as part of the fabled *Merrill's Marauders*. This simple man from Indianapolis was soon thrust in the middle of some of the most intense fighting of the South Pacific, assigned to operate a .30 caliber machine gun against heavy Japanese resistance. The Japanese would usually attack at night and my uncle would unload his weapon into a sea of tracer fire, unsure of whom he was actually shooting at. In the morning he would awaken to a field of dead Japanese soldiers.

Over a plate of eggs and buttered toast, he recalled how when night fell, so much changed for the soldiers of the Burma conflict—a kind of comfort to chaos. The sounds of Japanese military vehicles clanging on the cobblestone Burma Road would cause a call to man the .64 caliber mortars. Al and his platoon would rain down a barrage of exploding ordinances toward the sound of the convoys, leaving burned-out Japanese vehicles and the accompanied dead to line the road. Many nights he spent hunkered down in foxholes only to awaken and find that incoming artillery had missed his hole by only a few feet, sparing him from certain death.

"Uncle Al, were you scared? Did you think about dying?" I inquired, looking into his face for a sign of fear or regret that I never saw.

"Noooooo," he laughed. "I never even thought about getting killed myself. It just didn't cross my mind."

"What about the Japanese prisoners, how were they treated?"

"There were no prisoners . . . we killed them all," he replied matter-of-factly. "We killed them all."

In some ways he seemed to have a sense of nonchalance about death, when it came to the survivors. They were just hell-bent on doing their job: showing up, saving the world, and getting the hell back home. Uncle Al, like many of the old-time vets, just walked through life with an attitude of 'If it's my time, it's my time'. They were there to do their duty, to fight for a greater good, and their lives were expendable to achieve it. And if they survived, it was all the better.

After the war, Uncle Al found himself back in Indianapolis. He did not capitalize on the GI Bill and enroll in college, something I think he regrets. Instead, he settled down. In 1950 he married Becky, the girl he met at a bar-mitzvah in Cincinnati. They raised two children: a daughter, Sandy; and a son, Larry. With the help of his father, he opened a small grocery store on the near west side of Indianapolis (near 30th and Rader). It was a predominantly white, middle-class neighborhood. But in time that would change, and he would become the only white grocer in the middle of a working-class, predominantly African-American neighborhood. A Pepsi Cola sign with its dark letters, "Profeta's Market", stood out on the white cinder block and black tarpaper-roofed store. As the years passed, Al and his wife Becky along with their children became valuable members of the community. He kept his prices fair and low, often providing credit to the neighborhood poor. He lived a simple life and enjoyed simple pleasures. Having survived the war, I think he felt, as did most vets, that the rest of his life was like a free dessert. I'm sure he also felt that he had dodged all the bullets and bombs he would see this lifetime. On Halloween night, in

October of 1963, he found out he was horribly mistaken.

The *Holiday on Ice* show was in town and Uncle Al, Becky, and their two children had tickets. It was at the Coliseum, still a fixture of the Indiana State Fairgrounds. The show was enjoyable but Larry, then twelve years old, was upset that they were seated so high up. Larry noticed that there were empty seats down lower and implored his parents to move down. I think Al thought it was like cheating and wouldn't let him. Besides, he had paid for these seats. They stayed put and stayed alive.

For the 4,000 or so spectators, it was a graceful exhibition of the art of figure skating: smooth, seamless, and free flowing. Toward the end of the show, two explosions—caused by a leaking propane tank in a concession stand that blew up—sent bodies and severed limbs flying though the air. This turned the white ice into a frozen lake of charred human remains, concrete, and blood. Until the smoke cleared, Al and Larry thought it was all part of the show, some odd pyrotechnics. In all 74 people died and 400 were injured. The vast majority of the dead and injured came from the section where Larry had wanted to sit and had begged his father to move to earlier, the rows which now lay strewn with the mangled and the dead.

As they exited the Coliseum, they passed a man lying near the exit whose legs had been blown off. And for a moment, I can imagine Uncle Al felt he was back in Burma dodging bullets and ducking for cover. They found a young boy crying hysterically at the entrance. They took the child's hand and walked all around the Coliseum trying to find his parents. In time, they were found living and healthy. The reunion was emotional as expected. Al reflected very little on his near miss with death: He went on with his life. Grateful to be alive, he returned to the responsibilities at hand: raising his children, being a good husband and a good Jew, and running an honest business.

I loved it when Dad would take me to his store. I was amazed at how he seemed to know everyone's name that came into his small grocery. He would always be engaged in sarcastic banter with his customers. It was so clear to me, even then as a child of nine or ten, that everyone liked . . . no, loved this man. He had this old potbelly stove at the entrance. The wooden floors smelled like cold meat fat, and there was one of those pop machines as you entered that had a tall line of glass bottles. You put your coins in and pulled at the rough bottle top with a great deal of force to remove the sodas from the rollers. If successful, you were rewarded by an ice-cold grape or orange Nehi; it was frigid, frosty, and very satisfying, much like my Uncle Al.

For years, Uncle Al ran this small dilapidated store, scraping out a living that he supplemented by running numbers and buying and reselling lottery tickets from Illinois; something that, in all honesty, served as a form of entertainment for the community. Even though the neighborhood experienced the ravages of urban decay, drugs, and crime, he chose to stay and fight the good battle. The honest, hard-working people in the area depended on him for their groceries and the simple home supplies and hygiene items of everyday living. The big grocery chains weren't climbing over each other to build in the area, and most of the people relied on public transportation to get them to and from work, and to their doctors and banks. Having to take the bus for a simple carton of milk would have been both expensive and inconvenient. But they could walk to his store, interact with their neighbors and feel part of a community, of something greater than themselves. It was not just Profeta's Market; it was Everyone's Market. But in 1981, all of that changed when three men from Chicago shot Uncle Al, beat up his son, and robbed the store and the neighborhood of two of their most prized assets: my uncle and their market.

"This is a hold-up . . . open the safe," they shouted, pointing guns at my uncle and cousin who were the only ones in the store at the time. Uncle Al actually laughed. "What safe? We hardly have any cash, even by the end of the day." He smiled defiantly.

A friend had heard the commotion over an open phone line and notified the police. They were there in minutes, surrounded the store, and called the robbers out. Unfortunately the robbers panicked; one of them pushed my uncle to the door as a human shield, telling the police to get back. Then, for no reason at all, in clear view of his own son, he shot Uncle Al in the side with a .357 magnum revolver. The bullet passed clear through him, knocking him to the ground. This good man who survived WWII, an explosion at the Coliseum, was now dying on the floor of his own store in the middle of America's heartland thousands of miles from the Burma Road.

The police lobbed teargas into the small store, and the robbers eventually fled the building. They were arrested. Al was evacuated by medics to one of the regional trauma centers; he told the paramedic that he didn't think he was going to make it. I suspect the medic probably thought the same thing.

I was in high school when this occurred. I was called out of my classroom and told to go home right away. On my way I flipped on the radio, WIBC to be exact, just in time to hear, "Profeta shot." I hit the gas and flew home. To my relief, both of my parents and sisters were in the driveway. A few hours later, we knew that all would survive; it was a tremendous relief.

I am convinced that this man is unbreakable. Not only did he survive, but the .357 caliber slug missed all his vital organs as it passed clean through him. However, it did leave him with nerve damage, some chronic pain, and was enough of a disability that he could not carry on as the neighborhood grocer. Larry tried to maintain the store, but the work and frustrations of a small grocery were just not worth the effort. Thus, these three outsiders, who knew nothing of this man and his community, ended up stealing from everyone who lived there. Two years later, with a mixture of sadness and relief, Al closed the shop, gave all the food away to his former customers, and walked away with his memories and his life.

Al is an amazing man. I am not sure there is anyone who appreciates being alive as much as he does. His face is almost frozen in a permanent smile. I tried to mimic it once, and it hurt my face. My facial muscles have just not been cut and chiseled with the same degree of life optimism as his, though I am still trying to exercise those muscles on occasion.

Uncle Al is still living and kicking at age 82. He told me his goal is to be the oldest living WWII vet. He recently drove his car underneath a semi-trailer, shearing off the roof; but, of course, he walked away without a scratch. He works a few shifts in the old neighborhood at one of the area liquor stores and sees some of his former customers. Once a week he has lunch with the detective that pulled him from the store. He works out a few times a week at one of the local health clubs, and every Sunday you can find him and his friends, of which there are many, bantering about at Bob Evans Restaurant over breakfast.

A few years ago, Al buried his wife. When he talks about her, he still cries. I ask him if he has any regrets in his life and he says, "Just one: that my wife is not alive." Her passing, his wartime experience in Burma, almost dying on the floor of his market, and the Coliseum tragedy, all seem seemed to have led to one of his more intriguing activities. Al has taken on the sacred role of cleansing the bodies at the local Jewish funeral home, one of the greatest mitzvahs (good deeds) in Judaism. Why is it such a good deed, you may ask: because the dead cannot thank you. It is a wonderfully gentle and fulfilling deed. I have done it myself. You bathe and clean the body, scraping and removing all the dirt; you chant the customary prayers that have been recited for thousands of years, gently wrapping the hands, the feet, and the body in soft white cotton cloth. It is a very pure, gentle, and fulfilling offering. I think it's his way of thanking God for life, giving back to a God that has given him so much and has spared his own life so many times.

One of my favorite recurring questions asked in the ER is:

"Profeta . . . are you related to Al Profeta?" It is typically an older African-American patient or their family.

"I am," I reply. "Did you use to live near 30th and Rader?"

They always smile and say, "Sure did, used to go to his store." This was followed by, "Good man," or "How's his wife?" and "What's his son up to?" Or perhaps, "I remember when he was shot . . . what a shame." Then, of course, it's always followed by "Ask him if he remembers . . ." or, "Tell him I said hello."

I always look at them and give them an exaggerated, squinty-eyed smile and ask, "Don't I look like him?"

They always laugh and say, "Yeah, you do . . . you sure do." That's one of my favorite complements, one of the things I am most proud of in my life . . . being Al Profeta's nephew.

Chapter Eighteen

It Doesn't Take a Brain Surgeon to Raise a Child

I hate soccer. Mind you, I appreciate the athleticism, the strategy, and the endurance required to play the game, but I still hate watching it. I think what turns me off to the sport is the animated, rolling around in sham-agony that accompanies the attempts to draw a yellow card or red card or credit card, whatever they give out. Can you imagine what the sports writers in this country would say if our professional football players writhed around on the turf like that every time they were tackled? The fans would crucify them. Imagine how Yankee fans would act if after getting hit on the arm by a pitch, Johnny Damon fell to the ground, grabbed his hair, curled up in a fetal position, only to have two guys with a vintage World War II stretcher haul him off to the dugout. He'd have the crud beat out of him the first time he set foot in a Bronx bar.

Having an ER doctor for a parent must be tough on my kids. I don't get too alarmed, and after a busy day of listening to other people's complaints, the last thing I want is to hear the same noise at home. But alas, that's part of being a parent....right? I know that sounds kind of harsh and maybe a bit uncaring, but I am sure I am not alone. I'm certain many people with stressful jobs—the police officer, the school teacher, the guy that polishes the nuclear warheads—have a hard time putting it away and changing hats. I'm one of those. But my field of medicine offers a unique insight into the mind of an injured child.

When it comes to children, my own included, I feel that I have always understood the psychodynamics in relation to injuries. When a child stumbles and falls, the first thing they do is stop and look back at the parent, searching for clues as to how they are to respond to the injury. "Hey, Mom...are you looking...should I cry?" they say with their eyes. Most of the time it seems the child won't even react unless the parent responds. If the parent leaps with panic, the child will do the same. If the parent looks away, or doesn't make a big deal out of it, neither will the child.

Show me a child whose parent always rushes over, kneels to the ground with a great degree of frantic animation, showering sympathy and comfort on a kid with a penny-sized abrasion to their knee, and I'll show you a soccer player who rolls around on the grass, a baseball player who cries each time they strike out, or a basketball player who pouts about not getting the ball. Show me that parent and I'll show you an inconsolable child with a half-inch scalp laceration, a screaming child with a sprained wrist, a terrified child with an earache, an obstinate child who will not take their medication, a child whose next visit to the ER will be as terrifying as watching *The Exorcist* in a dark closet; because they have been denied the opportunity to learn self-control.

Show me a child who is sheltered from failure, who always has to be paired with their friends on the winning team, who gets a huge applause after striking out so as not to have their feelings hurt, and I'll show you a teenager who will be on Prozac by age fifteen. Show me a child whose parents sit for hours on end, hovering over their child as they do their homework, and I'll show you a college dropout, a young girl with an eating disorder, a teenager on Ecstasy, or a juvenile alcoholic. Show me a parent who runs interference with every student-teacher or student-coach conflict, and I'll show you a child with chronic fatigue syndrome, migraine headaches, fibromyalgia, and chronic absenteeism. Show me a parent who arranges play dates, and I'll show you a child who does not know how to make friends. Show me a parent who arranges for their children to be in every specialized sports camp and travel team because they feel their child needs it to compete, and I'll show you a child who will be kicked off his high school team for drugs, alcohol, grades, or attitude. Show me a child who is given everything their friends have, and I'll show you a child who will grow to appreciate nothing, who will talk back to nurses, teachers, physicians, and those trying to help during times of crisis. Show me this parent and I will show you a child who will not visit them in the nursing home, who will move far away once grown, who will be nothing more than a next of kin on a nursing home sheet or a phone call from a state a thousand miles away. These are the observations of an ER doc.

As a parent, I feel my responsibility js to balance comfort and love while at the same time teaching my children a sense of self-control and self-reliance. My wife and I made it clear to our kids at an early age: "If there is not a bone sticking out or blood squirting from a major artery, then there is no whining. If you fall from a bike, stumble on the sidewalk, drop from a tree, you are to jump up, stick your hands in the air, and yell, "Ta Da," as if it were all part of the show. I don't do homework. I did my time in high school, college, medical school, and residency.

"Son, I'll explain concepts to you but you better have exhausted all resources first. If there is a math problem wrong on your worksheet or a word spelled incorrectly, I'll tell you...just not which one. You can stay up as late as you like as long as there is a book in your hand...and no, the computer does not count as a book."

Now I don't know if that's the best way to raise a child, but I do know that it makes for a much quieter household, and lot less work. It's also pretty entertaining when you watch them crash their bikes, tumble ten feet, come up in a bloody mess, and scream, "Ta Da!", hop back on their bikes, and ride off. My kids don't get too upset about losing, striking out, or making mistakes. Their accomplishments are their accomplishments, not mine. Their failures are their failures...not mine. A while back my oldest son, Max, won the school science fair. What made me so proud was the fact I did not even know he had entered it. He did the entire project by himself at school. He went to the regional final and didn't win; that really upset him. He was angry and cried, and then told me there were tons of projects that could not have possibly been done by kids alone. He felt cheated. My response to him was the following: "Max...I could care less; quit whining and get over it. I would rather that you got last place with your own work than first place with mine.

I could not be any more proud of you than I am. Now get your shoes on and let's go shoot some hoops...oh, by the way, life is unfair...there, now didn't you learn a lot?"

He smiled and gave me a big hug. We grabbed a basketball and I proceeded to kick his butt in a little one-on-one. I haven't heard another word about the science fair since. By the way, when that kid finally beats me at hoops he'll know he has really won...so far, he's zero for about a thousand.

I like to think I'm parenting the right way for me. I've never had to pull my kid off the field because he cried on the pitcher's mound, missed a fly ball, and fell to pieces. They don't throw fits when they get their immunization shots, their teeth pulled, or hair cut. They still come into my room when they have bad dreams, cuddle up, and find respite next to their parents. In that manner, I never turn them away. I was scared to death of the dark when I was a kid, so I'm pretty lenient when it comes to those kinds of fears.

Though they each have their own rooms, I let them sleep pretty much wherever they want. For the most part, they sleep together in the same bedroom, though they jump around now and then. They find profound comfort in each other, between their constant fighting, of course, which I think is very important. My father grew up loving one brother and hating the other. My kids will love each other no matter what, even if I have to cut them out of the will to do it.

When it comes to sports and my children's accomplishments,

I am a realist. We are short Jews. Short Jews are destined to become intramural point guards, decent second basemen, punters and place kickers, good tennis players and golfers. Okay, so Dolph and Danny Shays made it in the NBA. There was Sandy Koufax, Rod Carew, and Mark Spitz, too. I also know people who smoked their whole life and never got lung cancer. In reality, the chances are better my kids will own an NBA franchise before they play for one; which is precisely why I don't understand parents today. I love sports, I mean I love them. I would watch celebrity goat herding if it were on television, I would even watch the French play soccer if I had to. But my own identity is not about my kid's fastball or jump shot.

I once took care of a high school football player, a freshman mind you, who was hit so hard his grandkids will be born concussed. He was hit all the way back to the first grade, horribly confused. Fortunately, his CT scan was negative and he did not suffer any life-threatening brain injuries. When I informed the father he would most likely not be able to play for the next few months, you would have thought I had told him the kid had metastatic bone cancer. I actually had to pause and rehash in my mind if I had said what I had thought...did he misunderstand me?

"You don't understand!" he cried and screamed at me.

"What don't I get?" I asked, very confused.

"He's a freshman!" he responded...more upset.

"He's a freshman...and...that means what?" I asked. He glared at me as if I should know where he was going. I didn't.

"He's a freshman on the varsity, the starting punter," he cried.

Now you might think this behavior is an anomaly; I assure you it is becoming more of the norm. I see children participating in sports at their parents' urging while still profoundly ill or injured. I've seen children pushing the envelope of weight loss and gain with parental approval. I've watched parents refuse to discipline a child for drugs, alcohol abuse, and truancy, all for the fear of losing a spot on the choir, band, cheerleading, or the football squad.

The ramifications are that we have created a generation of parents who are afraid to punish, put their foot down, and only serve to make excuses for their child's behavior. It is always someone else's fault: the crowd they run with, the bad kid down the street, the mean teacher, or the racist coach.

I used to tell my wife that a certain high school on the north side of Indianapolis was a statistical anomaly in which it was the only school in America where ninety percent of the kids were in the top ten percent of their class.

Every weekend it is the same story: the anorexic teen, the suicidal teen, or the depressed teen. "I want my son tested for drugs; I want my daughter tested for sexual activity. Someone gave her Ecstasy; someone gave him vodka."

I used to carry a card in my wallet for the parents. I would hand it to them if they started down the road of denial or excuses. It read:

He is in the top ten percent of his class.

She has never done anything like this before.

He is a good kid.

She has never been in trouble.

He is a great soccer player on the junior, national, regional... blah, blah, blah team.

She doesn't drink; someone gave it to her...blah, blah, blah.

He's never used drugs before; someone gave it to him...blah, blah, blah.

Most of the time they would hand it back, look at me, and respond, "Guess we're not alone...you're right, Doc, you're right." Sometimes they thought I was just being a prick so I stopped and let Social Services take over...it's easier that way.

I've never read a book on parenting. I do know that it doesn't take a brain surgeon to raise a child. I figure people have been doing it for what, 500,000 years or so, without too much trouble?

There are probably only a few basic rules that stand the test of time, anyway. Love them. Love them some more. Spend quality time with them. Be their parent first, their friend second, and make damn sure they understand the difference. Talk to them every day, and hug and kiss them every day. Make sure they understand they are the center of your life...and if they aren't, then make them the center of your life. Get them involved in volunteerism early, and teach them to respect you, God, and human dignity. But most of all, teach them to be self-reliant and instill them with confidence. Practice these things and they will honor you by being good people into adulthood and caring children when you can no longer care for yourself.

Chapter Nineteen

I'd Like to Buy a Casket for an Infant

The call for the code came over the hospital intercom, loud and mechanically, "Attention all personnel, Code One, the outpatient surgical waiting room." The voice repeated the message three times with a sense of panic behind the static.

"Can't be real?" I said. "Someone probably fainted coming in the outpatient surgery doors." (This is a patient area located on the other side of the hospital). Non-emergency personnel tended to freak out at the slightest upset or injury, so every lightheaded family member who sees a spot of blood becomes a major episode. Typically, it was grandma getting a bit winded walking in for a procedure, or dad fainting when his child got an IV. A Code One in that area of the hospital tended to be nothing urgent. The ICU was a different story, though. Those were always real.

"Well, let's go just in case," I said, motioning to one of the nurses. The ER staff was responsible for responding to all cardiac arrests in the hospital, so we quickly grabbed the code equipment and defibrillator and started running to the farthest spot from the ER, knowing with some certainty that it would be nothing big. We expected to administer a pat on the back, a check of the blood sugar, and a quick, "You'll be okay, let's get you back to the ER just to check you out." Was I ever wrong?

As I entered the long hallway leading to the outpatient waiting area, I could see a large crowd of white coats and blue scrubs in the distance. I was confused because everyone seemed to be standing up, not kneeling down like they normally would around a patient who has been helped to the ground. They were milling around a desk in the middle of the lobby, and most everyone looked frantic; some of the nurses were holding each other and crying. That's when I saw him.

He was blue, cold, and dead. CPR was ongoing; an anesthesiologist who was nearby had placed a small breathing tube into the infant's lung. Chest compressions were being performed by a terrified nurse, and another anesthesiologist, hands trembling, was hurriedly trying to get an IV in the child's arm. This certainly was not the norm for most of them. Their patients were usually alive and pink with big plump veins. A young Hispanic woman lay collapsed against the wall, cradled by hospital personnel. All eyes immediately fell on me to take control and save this infant— a task I immediately knew would be impossible.

I grabbed the defibrillator paddles and quickly applied them to the infant's chest to get a reading as to what this child's heart was doing, to see if there was any hope, though I already knew what I would find. I also knew it was important for all present to see the flat, straight linear tracing of a silent heart, so that there was no confusion for this crowd of onlookers. Still, I went through the motions.

"You, continue CPR, increase your rate; you, hyperventilate this infant; you, get me an interosseous needle out of the code cart! Pharmacy, get me out some epinephrine and atropine based on five kilograms [about ten pounds]!" Everyone jumped certain that this ER doc was going to save the day; a sense of false relief came over the crowd.

I quickly cleaned the child's leg and drove the interosseous needle into the soft bone marrow of the child's tibia so as to get quick access to the delicate circulation. I pumped fluid and drugs into this child in a futile attempt to salvage an infant who, in all practicality, had been dead for some time. But it was important, not only for the family but the entire staff traumatized by this event, to feel that everything possible was being done. We continued down this path with me watching the monitor, ordering medications, pumping fluids, checking breath sounds, going through the motions of playing doctor to a crowd who had no idea that there was no, and I mean no, chance of survival.

Forty-five minutes later, on a cold desk in the middle of the lobby with hordes of onlookers, gawkers, and hospital personnel, this child was declared dead.

By this time, Mom had been escorted to a waiting area outside of the lobby and was sitting with our clergy. I thanked everyone involved and covered the child with a small blanket, gently lifting him and placing him on a gurney. I reassured everyone that they could not have done anything different to save this baby, that this child was dead long before they had entered the wrong doors of the hospital. I think they found this comforting. Next, I walked through the surgery waiting room filled with the family members of other patients having various OR procedures. All of them were well aware of the goings-on outside the waiting room door. They all looked at me searching for the answer to the question: had the baby died? They saw the answer in my face. Many of them held each other's hands and quietly sobbed as I walked into the private consultation room off to the side.

Mom spoke no English, but I could speak Spanish fairly well. In the 1980s, pre-med programs pushed French, German, or Latin as the language of choice. Just for this reason, I was glad I chose Spanish. I had never treated a German or French national who did not speak English, and as far as I knew, Julius Caesar had yet to step foot in our ER. Learning Spanish had been a godsend and made me that much better of a physician: I even feel it should be mandatory today for all pre-medical students.

As expected, the mom had collapsed into a palpable despair that hung like a fog over the waiting room. It was thick and humid as we wheeled her and her dead child back to the ER. Dad showed up shortly thereafter and fell to the ground crying with heart-wrenching sobs of pure life-altering grief.

His name is Carlos, and I now consider him my good friend. It turns out that Carlos is one of the longtime bus supervisors and a short order cook at Sullivan's, my favorite steakhouse in the city. There was something about his despair, his absolute love for the small infant that hit me like a brick: It was how I felt about my children, and I felt his loss . . . I felt it deeply.

The clergy sat with the grieving parents and comforted them. By that time we had called the coroner and the funeral home. It turned out that this was most likely a classic case of sudden infant death syndrome, in which the child probably had a severe respiratory virus and had been bundled and put in the crib facedown, and most likely suffocated. The coroner did not feel that an autopsy was warranted, and thus, we could release the baby to the funeral home. I told the clergy that I wanted to help with the funeral and asked if he could get them on the line.

"Hello, my name is Dr. Profeta; I'm one of the ER physicians at St. Vincent Hospital. I would like to buy a casket for the infant who just died here. How much would that cost me?" The funeral director told me that if I would buy the casket, he would donate the plot and the stone. "You got yourself a deal," I told him. With that, I bought my first casket.

I didn't go to the funeral. I didn't even look for it in the paper. The clergy from the hospital officiated at the burial and filled me in on the event. I asked him not to tell anyone in the hospital; I was afraid people might think I actually had a heart. He told me the family was very appreciative of my generosity.

Perhaps four months went by until I finally worked up the courage to tell my wife that I wanted to go back to Sullivan's. I asked if Carlos was working, not wanting to startle him. The manager recognized my name and thanked me for helping Carlos (all the employees at Sullivan's like him and felt for him). Carlos visited our table and, in the middle of the restaurant, cried and hugged me. He told me how grateful he was for all I had done and informed me of the good news: his wife was pregnant again.

Since then, Carlos has been a guest in my home. He comes

with his wife and children and picks jalapeño peppers from my garden. We play basketball on occasion, and he has even cooked for me on my birthday. He tells my children what a great dad they have. His praise is really unnecessary, but I can tell it's his way of saying thank you; however, the occasional tuna sashimi appetizer is more than adequate.

What Carlos doesn't realize is that I am just glad that I can bear witness to the triumph of the human spirit. I am thankful that God has blessed Carlos and his wife with a young healthy son. I am grateful for the soft touch and kisses of my sons. With the patience of Job, this spiritual man who came to this country and struggled to pursue the American dream has found a new spirit. He has risen from tragedy, arisen from despair, and made me proud to be a part of his world.

Chapter Twenty

"You Gave Me Forty-eight Hours"

We do funerals better. I mean it. Jews know how to put on a good funeral. You die; you're in the ground in 24 hours—no embalming, no flowers; there is a simple wooden box, and you go home. Everyone comes to visit for the next week or so, and they feed you. I have always insisted what bothers me the most about dying is all the good food I would miss out on.

I feel uncomfortable at Christian funerals, and I admit it. I feel bad that families have to spend days cooped up in a foreign mortuary, away from their own kitchens, their bedrooms, their homes. They have to cope with their worst life tragedy in an alien world of garishly framed European prints, stenciled landscapes, and artificial flowers. They spend two or three days dressed in their Sunday best, standing in lines while throngs pay tribute in a well-choreographed reception line of gentle hugs, tilted heads, and 'so sorry's'. So when I decided as an after-thought to pay respects to the husband of a deceased patient who I treated in the ER, I was a bit apprehensive, and not just because it was a Christian funeral. I was afraid he might blame me for his wife's death.

CPR was ongoing when the medics brought her into the ER. They reported that she suddenly dropped while talking to her husband. He came in with the medics as they performed chest compressions, refusing to leave the room. It was around one or two o'clock in the morning, and she was our only patient. It was evident from his demeanor, his posture, the way he carried himself that he was someone who was used to being in control. Probably a well-to-do businessman from the north suburbs, the type that knows so and so, plays golf with you-know-who, and is the man with courtside seats. But that night he was out of his element; that night he was only a man about to lose his wife.

She kept going in and out of ventricular tachycardia and ventricular fibrillation. Her heart was beating at a rate so fast her brain failed to get enough blood. I kept administering shocks of electricity, and shots of lidocaine, bretylium, magnesium, and procainamide —anything to keep her in rhythm. I even tried to run a pacemaker, but to no avail. This went on for nearly two hours. And then, as suddenly as her soon-to-be-fatal heart rate had started, it slowed and began beating with the smooth regularity of normalcy. Her blood pressure stabilized and to the untrained eye she appeared fine, pink, and well perfused. He was so relieved when the nurse pronounced that her pulse was stable and her pressure good, and the oxygen was perfect. But I knew that her brain was dead, her soul was gone, and we were left with a beautiful shell of a previously vital woman who would never again hold the hand of her child, her husband, or her mother.

I tried to be quietly optimistic. "We have to wait, we'll get her down to the big house (our other hospital), and we'll see what happens over the next few days. It's too early to tell how much, if any, brain damage she may have suffered."

"Then we need to hurry, get her moving. Let's go, let's get her transferred, Doc." I let him take some control, make some phone calls, and be a player. Mr. So and So showed up with his wife, dressed in pajamas, looking nothing like the imposing figure of corporate hierarchy that he portrayed in public. They came as simple friends awakened in the middle of the night by the pleas of someone they loved. They stood to the side and let the chips fall; the transport team came and gently slipped from the ER in the wee hours, with their friend in tow.

She died 48 hours later, her husband and family by her side. As I drove home a few days later, I passed the funeral home that served as her final open house. I had never called on a former patient, since ER doctors are footnotes in their lives. We are the ten-minute silent heroes, whose names never stay on the tongues of those who seek our charge, our responsibility. We are not invited for dinner, given tickets to games, or offered use of condos in Vail. We show up, do our job, and fade into the background from whence we came.

Though I didn't know her or her husband, I was somehow drawn to the funeral home. I tried to drive past but the wheel turned itself, the car slowed, and I parked alongside the façade of Someone and Brothers. The parking lot was packed with Bavarian vehicular opulence, and I immediately felt a stranger. I was dressed in jeans and a brown Avirex bomber jacket, completely out of my comfort zone amongst the black suits, dark glasses, and shades of grey. I filed into the line watching, listening, and approaching the man as he stood next to her casket. It seemed a sea of sterile handshakes, one after another, gentle pats, tilted heads, and 'so sorry's': one after another, one after another. I could feel the inquisitive eyes of his family and friends on me, wondering who I was. As he shook hands with the grey suit next to me, he glanced in my direction with a look of confusion. He did not know me. He talked with the grey suit some more, and then suddenly stopped cold, looking at me again. He dropped the grey hand and turned to me, putting both arms on my shoulder, and pulled me close to him. His eyes filled with tears, he could barely breathe.

"You gave me 48 hours with my wife that I would not have otherwise had, and for that I am eternally grateful."

I may be born into a thousand lives, live a million years, and see a billion sunsets, and this will always remain one of the most comforting, sincere, and gracious things ever spoken to me. I have had a few years to reflect on this event and in no uncertain terms, I feel the same about my own wife, my own children. Every minute of every day that I can have them near and that I can hold them is that much more special. My children push me aside at times, overwhelmed with the hugs and kisses. But one

thing is for sure; when I die, I want my epitaph to read:
"Here lies Louis; he used up his allotment of hugs and kisses."

Chapter Twenty-one

F.O.P.

My initials are LMP (Louis Mark Profeta). It is monogrammed on my briefcase. Unfortunately, in medical jargon, 'LMP' also stands for 'last menstrual period'. You will find it on all of our charts. I have patients who are routinely SOBs...or 'short of breath'. They frequently go long periods of time without having BMs, or suffer acute MIs due to CAD, PEs, CVAs, TIAs, SBOs, or DVTs. Some go through DTs since they can't get ETOH. We get EKGs to rule out VT, SVT, LVH, WPW, or IHSS. I order EEGs, CTs, MRIs, TEEs; place IVs and CVP lines; do LPs; and provide O2. We give TPA, MS, LR, or D5W, often by IVP in hopes of being able to DC them ASAP. Unfortunately, they often end up getting a PTCA, CABG, or TAHBSOs in the OR after leaving the ER. Many end up in the ICU if they are not OK. Occasionally, though, they arrive DOA... UC? I love taking care of all sorts of patients...except one type...the F.O.P.

In most ERs 'F.O.P' stands for one thing: 'full of poop'. In our ER, it means something else...'friend of Profeta'. I grew up on the north side of Indianapolis, a city of about one million people. My parents grew up here, as well as my wife's family, all of our uncles, aunts, and so on. The Jewish community is small: about three to 5,000 people. Because we can mostly pretend to trace our roots back to Abraham and Sarah, they all think they're related to me. And if there is one thing we Jews are good at, it's working the system; whether it's getting dinner reservations, Pacers tickets, or being bumped to the front of the ER triage line.

Now, if you take those individuals aside, and then add all of the other people I know from my neighborhood, and the forty years I spent growing up here and attending high school just down the street, sprinkle on my kids' school, sports, my parents' friends, my siblings' friends, and throw in one degree of separation for another 2,000 individuals, that makes a solid seven to eight thousand people that know me directly or indirectly....and they all live within about ten miles of our ER. I have never worked a single shift in our ER where I have not cared for someone that I have known. It has become so routine that our ER has created its own acronym...F.O.P.: 'family (or friend) of Profeta'. One Christmas party, or should I say, 'holiday party', as my partners call it, so as not to make me feel isolated, the nurses gave me a faux hotel guest registry book.

I love my family and friends, don't get me wrong, and there was a time that I enjoyed the notoriety, but let me paint a picture for you: I work a ten- to twelve-hour, brutally tense and stressful shift. I come home exhausted, hoping to spend some downtime with my family, only to be met by a pile of messages to call 'x', 'y', and 'z' about their health questions.

"Ms. Schwartz's daughter is in town and has a sore throat. Can you call her in..."

"Martin down the street has a question about which orthopedist..."

"Your mom wants to see if you can get the results of her pap smear..." and on and on, and on.

Early in my career I made the mistake of opening myself up to all this, by being approachable. I have to admit...the reasons were not always admirable. I was always searching for the angles and the favors, but mostly I loved the attention and the affection that helping these people brought me. I would do a favor, see their kid, etc...and they, in a sense, owed me one. I have never been really good at making friends, and this somehow filled the void. It made me feel needed and loved. This is what some insecure people do. Other physicians may become raving tyrants, highly overestimating their own self worth....this was never my style. I knew I was insecure, I just didn't know how to fix it....time and age just sort of worked it out. Now I'm mostly just a temperamental prick... albeit an honorable one.

However, I was left with a dilemma: The medical favors and accessibility for the myriad that felt they could call me on my free time no longer did anything for me other than take up my time. Once I became content with my lot in life and secure in who I was, I did not need this attention, and in some cases, it left me feeling taken advantage of, taken for granted. Worst of all, many times the individual tossing my name around like a tennis ball was really not that close of a friend. Even worse, they would interject my name around in a manner that was disrespectful to the other doctors or nurses caring for them.

"If you don't hurry up and get me to X-ray, I'll tell Dr. Profeta."

"I'm very good friends with Dr. Profeta, and he said to make sure x, y, and z is done."

All of this verbal garbage on their part was always pure bullshit, but in the beginning, many times, the nurses were unaware of this. I had to literally tell them, "If the individual is really that good of a friend they would have called me at home and I would have relayed a message, or come to the ER myself." I told the nurses to simply hand the phone to the patient and tell them to call me at home. Very rarely has a patient taken the bait....usually the F.O.P.s shut their mouth. On a couple occasions I had to lay the law down to some so-called F.O.P.s, and tell them where they really stood on my friendship scale and let them know they were never to use my name again. Usually, these F.O.P.s were seeking drugs or causing some other problem in the ER. I assure you, there are no classes in medical school on how to deal with this...you're on your own; besides, I'm not sure physicians in academia have friends anyway.

What has confused me even more is this: How do you handle social situations when you are intimately familiar with the patient/friend's inner personal problems? As would be expected in any cross section of our society, there are issues with drug abuse, HIV status, depression, alcoholism, spousal abuse, infidelity, and a myriad of illnesses and neuroses that permeate our culture. My position simply brings them to light in these F.O.P.s. I have had to sign commitment orders, pump the stomachs, do pelvic or rectal exams, treat sexually transmitted diseases for people I consider friends and good acquaintances. Unfortunately, I have also had to pronounce some of them dead. It goes with the territory I guess, but it makes for uncomfortable Christmas open houses, Fourth of July celebrations, and even foursomes of golf.

A few years ago, the situation was so out of control that I snapped and requested....no, demanded...that my wife stop making friends.

"I have enough friends. Every time we make more friends, I just have to start working harder. In fact, I want to downsize. I want an 'F.O.P. clearing sale'. I don't want to be invited to anything, and I don't want to meet anyone new. I just want to stay home, cook, watch TV, and play with the kids. Oh, and while we're at it, I am no longer answering the phone. You will play the role of triage nurse. If people call, just tell them I'm asleep, out of town, or recovering from a scorching case of herpes. In fact, use that excuse for all of them. 'I'm sorry, Dr. Profeta is recovering from a scorching case of herpes, but I'm sure he'll be happy to take a close look at your child's sore throat.'" Alas, if only I had herpes! I even felt myself wishing for herpes..."Honey, could I please get herpes for Hanukkah...after all, all of our friends have it...I know."

Still, my approachability and published phone number set the tone of being a doctor who can be relied upon to help out in a pinch, make special effort to see a friend, stop by their home, or have them stop by mine. I availed myself in the ER to abiding by their request to be seen only by me, instead of having a medical student or resident first examine them, and to do all the documentation, further increasing my workload in the department. I could be relied upon to call in a script for amoxicillin, or someone's hypertension medication, when their own doctor wouldn't call them back. Or I would simply make myself available for a second opinion when they would feel confused, ill-informed, or scared. There was a time when I relished this, but over the years it changed to feelings of emptiness. I was doing all of these favors, and to be honest, I could have cared less for the people I was helping. At times, I felt like a priest taking confession, offering counseling and support, while at the same time wanting to smash a brick over the head of the person sitting on the other side of the screen. I admit it. One day, it all caught up with me, so I did something I never ever do: I asked for help and confided in my neighbor and friend, Reid.

Reid is a fascinating individual. He went to school at Brown, the bastion of liberalism. When George Bush won the last election he went into a deep depression and threatened to move to Canada or Nicaragua. I, of course, tried to comfort him by turning his car radio to Rush Limbaugh, by inviting him to Republican fundraisers, and by putting 'Bush/Cheney' stickers on his car. I even carved a pumpkin in the silhouette of a large penis and put it in his front yard while he was on vacation. This was after he put a 'for sale' sign in my front yard with the number 696-6969 as the inquiry line. By the way, cars stopped in front of his house for two straight nights taking photographs of the pumpkin my three sons and I carved.

Reid may be the funniest, most entertaining person I have ever met, and he has become a great source of comic relief and a great friend. He is also one of those new age hippies/venture capitalists who has made a lot of money in the steel industry and has used his good fortune to start a charter school for the underprivileged, and a school and clinic in South America. He also does all of these cognitive psychology and group counseling session seminars. At times, I think he would be better suited for

Berkeley, since his ideology in the heart of Indiana sticks out like a rabbi in Saudi Arabia. He recommended the name of a cognitive psychologist to discuss my dilemma.

I decided, with much prodding, to give it a try. I attempted to 'peel off the proverbial layers of the onion', as the psychologists like to call them.

So I walk into the office, and bingo, I recognize the guy immediately....he exercises at the same place I do...go figure. So I sit down and get right at it.

"Doc...here it is...I help all these people, friends, relatives, and acquaintances....but I just don't give a fuck when it comes down to it. I hear their problems, their complaints, mind you on my free time, away from the hospital, and...I could just care less. For the most part I want to slap them across the face and tell them to stop whining. Funny thing is...I don't feel that way at work. There is a different set of dynamics there. I love, absolutely love my patients in the ER. I thrive there. I'm a different person. I get them coffee, blankets, anything to make their visit more pleasant. I truly want to help in the setting. But once I leave, man...I'm Mr. Hyde under a papal façade."

"Do these people that intrude on your free time know how you feel about taking the time to address their needs, to help them?" he inquired.

"No, I cover it up pretty well. That's why they keep coming back, I guess."

"Sure they do...you have been enabling their behavior. But let me ask you something...Is it really a huge burden on you, or is it something else that is bothering you? Perhaps the realization that you just don't empathize with their plight...you just help."

"No, it's not that big of a deal. To be honest, most everyone is very appreciative. Like I said, though, it's like, once I leave work an empathy switch goes off in me. Big deal, huge burden?...No...it's not that big a deal to me...to them it is. I just have no real feelings about them or their plight either way. I'm sure it would be different if they were real close friends or family with life-threatening problems. But most of this is just simple stuff ; offering reassuring words, making them feel important in the ER...what I like to call mental masturbation. I watch TV and I see all these commercials to sponsor some poor kid in the Sudan or El Salvador or in 'Who-gives-a-shit-istan' and the people seem so enriched to be doing what they're doing, helping, crying, looking so spiritually fulfilled..."

"...and once you leave the ER you still help the needy...just devoid of these same emotions you have at work," he inter-rupted. "Let me ask you something, Louis...which do you think is tougher?"

"What do you mean?" I inquired.

"Which is tougher...being charitable, availing yourself of time and energy because you have a deep-seated spiritual mission or emotional attachment to the cause, or doing the same without that feeling of religious or spiritual self-fulfillment?"

"The latter, I suppose."

"Hell yes, it's the latter. Besides, you need to turn that empathy stuff off sometimes, except perhaps for your family and those closest to you...understand?"

I smiled, understanding what he was getting at. The recip-ients of my benevolence were not dissimilar to those receiving mission aid in the Sudan. It made sense. God does not care how I feel about this, and for the most part, it doesn't cross the mind of the poverty-stricken child, my family, friends, and so on. They just need. It's not about me...it's about them. The starving kid doesn't consider the degree of spiritual enlightenment that seeps from the pores of the family in Lagotee, Indiana each time they sign and send that check. He just wants the clothes, the food, or a roof over his head.

Suddenly, I felt a huge sense of accomplishment and looked at myself in a whole new light. It would be so easy to render assis-tance on my free time if I truly had a spiritual motivation to perform these simple deeds, but all along I had been giving of my time regardless. I was giving just because that is what you are supposed to do, like holding a door for a stranger or thanking the waiter. Somewhere deep in my soul, in my very being, I was doing what was right regardless of my own personal feelings. Where it came from…I don't know. It certainly was a compilation of life experiences, good parenting, solid teachers, and role models sprinkled with a touch of the divine. So, for the first time in years, I stood a little straighter and thought to myself, "Maybe I'm not such a prick after all."

Chapter Twenty-two

The Tylenol Anniversary

I am not at all amazed at the longevity of some marriages. I am more amazed at how few marriages actually survive. It seems that so few people take their promises and commitments seriously. I love caring for patients where the husband and wife proudly proclaim fifty, sixty, even seventy years of marriage and devotion. It is even more gratifying when both still have their faculties into their eighth and ninth decades, and leave holding hands, arm in arm, caring for each other with the gentleness of a mother and child. The dynamics and interactions between spouses in the extreme age group are godly in the purest sense. There is unselfishness there that can be found nowhere else. It is a place where time stops, and the world only exists between the two of them—and I'm just some young tourist guide giving them directions on how to eke out a few more months or years, or simply how to get Herbert to pee more easily.

I know there are paper, wood, silver, gold, and diamond anniversaries, but I think there should be a Tylenol anniversary, too. It should be the 'get out of jail free card' of marriage. You're allowed one bad year every seven to ten, or so—a year when things don't go so well: perhaps with health, finances, or simple interpersonal relations. The Tylenol anniversary would come to symbolize all the headaches you caused each other over the past year. It would serve to acknowledge those aches and pains of growing together, all those lean moments when everything was not all roses. It would reflect those years when pain was more prevalent than passion, when fear was more common than faith. I think every marriage could use a year like that, unless of course you and your wife see the problems of life as just another opportunity to find closeness in each other's company. These partners need no help or panacea for what ails them; they just need each other, even if it involves months and years in the hospital.

I came to know Sandy when he was lying in the Coronary Intensive Care Unit of Presbyterian Hospital in Pittsburgh. I was on the medicine service that month and took care of the patient in the room next to him. Sandy was not my patient, but somehow I struck up a conversation with him and his wife, Arlene, quickly becoming fascinated with the undying commitment they had to each other. Sandy was a victim of what we call piss poor protoplasm. He just had bad genes.

Premature heart disease, though he had led a fairly healthy life, made him a victim of multiple heart attacks early in his thirties. This left his heart irreparably damaged, and now years later he was in need of a heart transplant. Unfortunately, his tissue and blood type made it quite difficult to find a donor, and he was too ill to wait at home. So, he lay in a hospital bed for months and months on end. At times, he was dependent on a balloon pump (a large plastic tube sewn into the main artery of the groin) to help his feeble heart maintain some semblance of function. He was sallow in color, always looking on the verge of death, and was a thin-waisted Nosferatu or vampirish shell of a younger man I always imagined him to be.

Amazingly, though, he never complained. He just loved being alive, even if living meant being confined to a geriatric chair and a hospital bed. Sandy always had his wife at his side, never leaving his room. She not only served as an extra caregiver but was his rooting section, his confidant, keeping his spirits up, imploring him not to give up, and fighting for each and every second she could spend with him. Weeks turned to months, coalescing into years with the same activity day after day.

Arlene would spend the night at the nearby Holiday Inn, arriving at the hospital early in the morning and leaving late in the evening, usually with no real news on when a donor would be available or what Sandy's chances were to find one. When I was at the hospital or on a service that brought me near the CCU, I would come by and visit. I even stopped in with my own wife once to introduce her to this amazing couple. Sandy was always so alert and engaging that it was hard to tell he was using up his last few heartbeats. Even when he was most ill, he always had a smile and was grateful to just have visitors, friends, and most of all, a spouse who was there, no matter what the time or day. Thus, when it came time for Arlene to leave his side for a few days, it was very hard and very emotional for both of them.

Their daughter was graduating from college—Cornell to be exact—and Sandy, who had been an English teacher in a previous life at Theodore Roosevelt High School in the Bronx, felt it was important for one of them to be there to celebrate this educational achievement. Arlene packed a small suitcase and hopped a plane at the exact moment that the heart donor, for which they had waited nearly seven months, was declared brain dead. Thus, the miracle for which they had been languishing for so many months was becoming a reality—a healthy heart for transplant into Sandy's dying chest. On the same day that his daughter would graduate from college, Sandy himself would graduate to the world of the standing and walking living.

It was around 2:00 A.M. when my wife and I were awakened by a phone call. Sheryl answered in a semi-sleep state. She heard a raspy voice on the other end of the phone. She quickly hung up, thinking it was a prank call. The phone rang again, and this time I answered.

"Louis . . . this is Sandy," the weak, hoarse voice called out to me.

"Sandy . . . what's up . . . what's going on?" I was surprised he was calling me so early. But there was a sense of urgency in his voice that said: this call is important.

"Louis . . . Arlene went out of town for our daughter's graduation, and wouldn't you know they found a donor . . . I'm going into surgery in about an hour . . . and if I don't make it . . . well, I wanted to thank you and Sheryl, and tell you how much I love and appreciate all you have done for me."

I was speechless for a second. My wife was listening in on the other line, her hand cupped over the receiver.

"Sandy . . . you'll be fine . . . I know it. I have all the faith that you'll pull through." I gave him a few more comforting words, and then gently hung up. Sheryl returned to the bedroom and put her arm around me.

"He's scared . . . poor guy, isn't he?" I nodded. "Well, you need to go in and see him off to surgery. I'll go with you," she said, imploring me with a small degree of her own excitement. I looked at her, knowing that she was exactly right.

We quickly threw on some sweats and hurried downtown to Presbyterian, arriving in the CCU just as they came to take him to the OR. A sense of relief and a smile crossed his face and filled the room. "You didn't think we'd let you go to surgery without wishing you good luck, did you?" I asked.

Tears filled his eyes. He could barely speak as he nodded and grabbed our hands with all the force his weakened body could muster.

"You'll be fine," I reassured him. "I'll be here when you wake up . . . both of us." And with that, gowned orderlies silently lifted his fragile frame onto the gurney, and they left for parts unknown.

We headed home to grab a few hours of sleep. I returned about six hours later to see Sandy in the postoperative ward. I remember thinking that even on the ventilator, with all the tubes and IV pumps, monitors, and lines attached to him, he looked better three hours after major surgery than he had in all of the time I had known him.

You could just see that the new heart was thunderously pumping blood to muscles, skin, and tissue that were barely being fed by his old diseased heart. He looked full, healthy, and pink. I knew he would see many more days.

Sandy's own father had died at age fifty-five, so Sandy held out in Pittsburgh until he was fifty-six just to be 'safe'. Shortly after his birthday, he gathered his belongings, clutched his wife to his new heart, and returned to the Bronx, to a home on a small street called Deb's Place.

A few more months passed before Sandy returned to see his physicians in Pittsburgh. He called me for dinner. When we met, I was struck by how tall he actually was. You see, I had never seen him standing up. He was strong and lean, having filled out his previously sagging skin and muscle bundles. He looked like a human being again. And as it was to be expected, Arlene clung to his side, so grateful to be in his presence, side by side — together. For six and a half years, Sandy did superbly, his borrowed heart beating strong in his chest. Unfortunately, as can happen, the anti-rejection medications took a toll on his kidneys. Once again, he found himself on a transplant list; this time it was for a new kidney.

The next six years were a mixture of treatment failures and successes, hospitalizations, surgeries, infections, and the accompanying laughter and tears, ultimately ending in his death. He spent a total of three and a half years in the hospital as his kidneys and finally his heart failed, and Arlene spent most of this time with him, save for the nights in the Holiday Inn.

"Do you think, if he could have done it all over again, would he have gone through the six years of dialysis, infection, pain . . . the treatment failures?" I asked Arlene after his death.

"Absolutely . . . why do you ask?" she responded, almost incredulous.

"Well, to be honest, most people would give up and say: I can't take this anymore . . . it's not worth it. I mean, did Sandy ever say this to you?"

"Never," she replied bluntly, without a hint of reservation.

"Why do you think that is?"

"Because he wanted to live; he wanted to be here for the children, and . . . he wanted to be here for me," she said, her voice cracking. "He once told me, during the three years of hospitalization and being the sickest, that they were some of the best years of his life, because we got to be so close and spend so much time together, just the two of us . . . you understand?"

I remained silent for a while. "I do . . . now."

A while back, I had major shoulder surgery and was confined to bed for two weeks, and I was unable to drive for a couple of months after that. I was dependent on my wife to feed me, bathe me, and drive me around town, and so on. It was humiliating on one level, but then I noticed how much extra time I was able to spend with her, and how much I needed her, not only for physical but for moral support. I appreciated how she was not only my partner in health, but in sickness too. I am thankful for those extra, inappreciable moments in time when it was just the two of us. We just celebrated our fifteenth anniversary by having dinner with our kids. I bought her flowers and a series of cards expressing my love and devotion. Even though it was a miserable year full of shoulder pain, surgery, and other maladies, I still think I'll hold off on cashing in on the Tylenol anniversary. Because, when it comes down to it, any year you get to spend with your wife and kids, no matter how bad it gets—well, that's a God-given gift, and a golden anniversary.

Chapter Twenty-three

Honor Thy Mother and Father

"Don't trust anyone over 30." This famous mantra of the 60s has created a generation-gap catastrophe that can be felt in every hospital, nursing home, and ER in America. The result is one of the hidden disgraces of modern society. These few words have given rise to a cultural chasm separating baby boomers and their parents, and now boomers and their children. It might account for more interpersonal angst than any phrase in America's history, which has left us on the verge of moral bankruptcy and has flooded our nursing homes with the not-so-dead as the dumping ground for those who just don't know how to care.

The chain of events is easy to follow. Somewhere around 1960 or so, a 40-year-old father gives his 18-year-old son some advice, the content of which doesn't matter. The 18-year-old son, who has been fed a diet of 'don't trust anyone over 30', tells dad to "go to hell," or "you don't know what you are talking about." Over the years, the 18-year-old son, or daughter, grows into a 40, 50, and 60-year-old. And because the seeds were sown for the 'I'm-smarter-and-wiser-than-you' weed, they never really develop the heart to heart, father to son, mother to daughter relationship that should end with child opening his home to the same parents that gave him or her life. They have not assumed the responsibility to nourish the very parents who fed them, clothed them, and nurtured them into self-sufficiency.

Instead of gradually and gracefully evolving into the role of the patriarch and matriarch of the family, they are thrust into that role by way of an illness or injury that robs mom or dad of their independence. Instead of slowly assuming the mantle, they kept a safe distance and then were suddenly appointed by way of a stroke, heart failure, mother's hip fracture or any one of a hundred illnesses or injuries that now put the 'burden' of care on the children. Sometime after 1990, the word 'burden' replaced the standard lexicon of 'responsibility', and parents went from being keepers of our pasts and guides of our future to problems we needed to sequester away in long-term care facilities.

So 80-year-old dad who fought in Normandy, and 80-year-old mom who rationed sugar and flour and sold war bonds are left to the impulsive healthcare whims of children who rarely make decisions greater than deciding: who picks Justin up at soccer practice, what color to paint the guest room, and should we opt for a 24- or 36-month lease? For thirty or forty years, these children have been removed from really talking, caring, and communicating with their parents. Grandma and Grandpa have simply become the home where one goes on the holidays. Once the baton was passed, they dropped it like a rattlesnake, right into the lap of the local ER or nursing home, and in its wake the spawn of the baby boomers is learning that the best way to care for their own parents is to have a nursing home on speed dial. The now grown-up boomer attaches a phrase like, "It's in their best interest," and ship mom or dad off to faux plantations with names like Sunny Acres, Oak Village Care, The Manor House, or Green Meadows.

Once the child said, "I don't trust you," the parent-child dynamic became something else, and the baby boomers became lost sheep in a wilderness of scrutiny. And for some forty years like Moses in the desert, they have been wandering and searching, and wandering and searching. And still they can't see that the answer to what they are missing lies not in a self-help book, or in a rerun of *Oprah*, but in the aging arms of their parents. For a while they tried to find comfort and solace in the country clubs, the PTAs, the soccer fields and baseball diamonds, and a host of after-school activities and overindulgences of their own children. But something predictable happened. Just around the time they insisted that the friends of their children call them by their first names, their own kids looked at them and said, "I don't trust you." So what did the boomers do? They finally turned to talk to their own parents only to find that their eyes had slowly failed, their minds were not as sharp, and the passing years had faded from their memory. Once their own kids left for college, or fled to go backpacking across Costa Rica, they found themselves alone, usually in marriages that barely represented what their parents had.

My grandmother lived under my parent's roof for some forty of her 94 years of life. She had her own small kitchen that she would stink up with burnt fish and onions. On the stove sat a small copper Turkish coffee pot, blackened and scorched by years of thick coffee. In her later years, she would forget my name, pass gas in public, forget to shave her facial hair, walk around the house in a bra, but I loved every minute of it (except the whole bra thing). She died with us holding her hand, in the comfy recliner that had become her bed for the three months preceding her death.

I know that there will be all sorts of excuses for why this arrangement will not work for some. Mom is too sick, dad won't feed himself, she can't walk without assistance, etc., etc., etc. Well, you can justify any sin, of omission as well as commission, if you try hard enough. When it comes to caring for elderly parents, people are only limited by two things: creativity and drive. There are, however, a few ground rules that need to be agreed upon beforehand to ensure that the transition is seamless. The most important being: when you stop eating, you will die. This is the necessity that all physicians understand, but most ignore and bury in the recesses of their treatment plans.

If you sign the papers to put a G-tube or feeding tube in your 80-year-old mother with Alzheimer's or other severe dementia because she is no longer eating, you will probably have a fast track to hell. I'm not taking about midway up the ladder to purgatory; I'm speaking of medieval inquisition hell. There is a special place in hell for sons and daughters who allow this to happen to the people who brought them into this world, nurtured them, rocked them to sleep, and held them to their breast during thunderstorms. There is a special place in hell for those who pop holes through the belly wall of their parents, shove plastic tubes in their stomach, and fill their intestinal tracks with a blended mixture of soy formula, Ensure, wheat germ, and sedatives. Because no one dies without a feeding tube, they die with them. The elderly will stop eating when it's their time; forcing them to eat is a desperate attempt to salvage our time. Certainly there are exceptions to this rule. But this is the reality of a huge number of terminally elderly that are planted in a bed and fed like hothouse tomatoes, instead of being allowed to die in dignity. The boomers have placed them on dialysis, put plastic tubes in their lungs, catheters into their groins and bladders, wrapped them in diapers and called it "love," then scurried off to tennis lessons and personal trainers.

There is a special place in hell for those who, instead of holding the hands, and gently rocking those they love to sleep, instead choose to watch them wither away while feeding a mind that long ago died.

So how do you convince a son or daughter to take them home, hug them, love them, clean them, feed them, and allow them a chance to pass away a little sooner in a family home? I'm not sure, but letting them know it's OK to die this way may be a start. It's OK to forgo a year in the nursing home for six months in the spare bedroom. Once those simple two letters are taken to heart, then all the pressure is off, and you can begin a wondrous journey of spiritual reconnection and reconciliation.

There is so much that's right in a family that takes in their parents. When they come to the ER, you can just see what a labor of love it really is for them. There is nothing more honorable, loving, and all-encompassing of God than that. Certainly it requires work and sacrifice. It will, however, strengthen the bonds of the entire family. It will bless your own children with the opportunity for them to be entwined with their ancestral past and that is as godly as it gets. There are so many more lessons to learn from these difficult acts of loving, kind nurturing, than from any other after-school activities. My mother took my grandma, her mother-in-law, into her home and cared for her for nearly 40 years. This is an absolute 100% free pass to heaven. While at times it was hard, she will tell you that she misses her every day and would do it all over again.

If it comes time for my mom or dad, my mother or father-in-law to need a helping hand, my door will be open, the bedroom will be made, the bathtub will be modified, and the recliner will be ready for them.

Chapter Twenty-four

From the Mouths of Babes

Over the last few years I have come to appreciate how much my children love to come to the ER and visit me while I work. There are many factors involved. Apart from them just wanting to come and see their dad, I know they relish the attention lavished on them by the staff. Also, I truly believe there is a component of pride, though they do not recognize it as such, in watching their dad work to save lives. I overhear them in conversations with their friends or in their school writings:

"My dad saves lives."

"My dad helps people."

"Daddy...'Mrs. So and So' said to say hello, and that you took care of her dad, her mom, her husband, her son..."

They will occasionally hold bandages while I splint, push a wheelchair for a nurse, or get a patient a blanket. I believe that these are the simple things that teach human compassion and respect. They teach a sense of responsibility for our elderly, a responsibility to the past. I watch these scenarios play out in public when my children hold a door for strangers, help with a grocery cart, or perhaps pick up a dropped glove. I try to teach my medical students that this is the true gold of being a doctor. It is not so much the skill, though it helps; it is the simple smiles, the attention to comfort, and an understanding nod or a comforting hand.

I must start by saying I love watching the faces of the nurses, medical students, and patients light up when these three precocious and, at times, inappropriate kids clamor into an already tense environment. You can quickly see and appreciate the change in dynamics in an instant. Everyone seems to slow down a bit, catch their breath, smile. The familiar phrases of "How's school?" or "Coming to see your daddy?" and "Hey, did you bring all of us food, too?" fill the air. It is in all regards celestial music in a brutal setting. That is, of course, until they open their mouths...then all bets are off .

An elderly lady sits lying on gurney, her eyes focused as Eli, then six, passes by. He stares intently at the web of lines and tubes snaking across her arm, and, of course, as most do, she flashes a conciliatory though somewhat strained smile to my child. The type of smile that says, "I was you once."

"What's wrong with that old lady?" Eli asks, his voice slightly broken with the plight of innocence. "She's sick," I replied. My arm encircled his shoulder in a futile attempt to ease his concern. "We are trying to make her better."

He looked back at me with deep, inquisitive, questioning eyes...the eyes of a child...going on thirty. "If she's sick, how come she's smiling so much...can I get a Coke now?"

So it seems God does have a sense of humor. I think it was his way of telling me to lighten up...the kid's only six. He has a whole lifetime to learn human compassion. These are the words from God's mouth to Eli's mouth to my ears. What sweet music...the music of innocence.

Chapter Twenty-five

"Hey Buddy . . . You Don't Belong Here"

It did not make a whole lot of sense to me at the time. Looking back now, it still doesn't. The man was in his seventies and had managed to scale the bracing of one of the many steel-girder bridges dotting the Pittsburgh area. Just prior to my arrival in the physician response vehicle, a fully equipped Jeep Cherokee loaded with rescue equipment, he took a header and plunged into the cold, murky water of the Monongahela River. A couple of fishermen in a small aluminum boat found the dead man floating on the river and towed his body to shore, where we could then drag him up on the bank. His pale eyes and mottled facial complexion were obscenely covered with river sludge and plant debris. On his chest, like a misplaced toe tag adhered to his rigor skin, lay beige and dimpled, a nitroglycerine patch.

Sometime in the last few hours, this gentleman got up, ate breakfast, perhaps combed his hair and took a shower, put on his nitro patch, and scaled the bridge with the intention of killing himself, and he succeeded. The paradox was unmistakable: a lifesaving medication on the body of someone who had just committed suicide. It told me that during this brief period of time there was a conflict in this man's heart between wanting to live and wanting to die.

I've heard it said that nearly every survivor in their final leap from the Golden Gate Bridge regrets their action during the fall to the bay below. I think it is because in those four intense seconds they come to realize that all their life's problems can be rectified, while their death will be permanent. I never know what to say to the survivors, be it from a gunshot wound, single-car motor vehicle accident, overdose, carbon monoxide attempt, or just the simple 'ten Tylenol gesture'. Every encouragement seems so clichéd, each word of comfort so rehearsed, so I say the same thing each time. "As bad as it is now, is how good it can be in the future. Besides, you have all of eternity to be dead and only one chance at being alive, so why not milk it for all it's worth?" It usually elicits a snicker that seems to say "never thought of it that way."

When it comes to successful suicides, the anger and despair on the faces of loved ones are beyond description. While all unexpected deaths are horrible, a suicide is perhaps the worst of all. The ones left behind are not only faced with the realization that the person they cared about is gone, but also that person was not who they thought they were. The dead take on a different persona. They are no longer remembered as the loving husband, the doting mother, or the tender if troubled teenager. They become something else. The loving husband, who did not love enough to stay with her and the children; the doting mother, who let her children bury her; the teenage boy, who left his loving sister with a lifelong burden. They become the hyphenated dead, the family footnote. They not only kill themselves, but they slash at the memories that others once held dear, akin to finding out a parent is a child molester, or a brother is a killer. This is the reality of suicide.

In these situations I have witnessed parents pulling out their hair, spouses physically punching the dead body in anger, children throwing furniture into the wall. Their despair goes beyond simple loss and instead morphs into incomprehensible ferocity at the source of their bereavement. They become the most upset at the ones whom they loved the most. Perhaps this is the reason why in traditional Jewish lore, the suicide victim is buried on the fringes of the cemetery, away from the other graves. It is as if the rest of the faithful dead are saying, "You do not belong here; you did not honor your gift on earth." And while it may seem cruel to the surviving family members, on some level I suspect it serves a greater purpose. It reaffirms to the living that the sanctity of life is undeniable, and our commitment to its preservation should never waver.

Chapter Twenty-six

Bowl Away

It never ceases to amaze me how people respond when someone dies in public, or when they witness a severe trauma or become privy to a very ill individual. It can run the gamut from a sense of profound sadness and sympathy to a response that is nothing short of being inconvenienced and lacking all semblance of human decency or class. There are the gawkers, the criers, the screamers, and the prayers. There are the helpers, the hinderers, the ambivalent, and the idiots. I have even witnessed parents hauling young children over to the scene of a catastrophe, keeping moronic voyeurism alive in the family. I've seen all of these people at some time in my career and often all of them at the same event.

Over the years I've kept my perspective while on the street; I try to help without intruding and make sure I leave when I'm not wanted. I've stopped at many accidents with my children, and I have always made sure that they are out of the line of fire and especially the line of sight. Unfortunately, they have been exposed through direct contact, stories, or dinnertime banter to situations only adults should hear. I worry about them at times, but they seem well adjusted. I'm trying to keep them as children for as long as I can, but it's hard these days.

A few years ago at a major league baseball game, the umpire suddenly stood up, backed away from the plate, and fell over dead due to a sudden heart attack. Medics, fans, and players worked feverishly to save his life but were unsuccessful. I anticipated that there would be a moment of silence, some sort of long delay, before some schmuck got on the intercom and made a typical generic comment about, "Well, I'm sure Umpire Bob would have wanted us to play on." Instead, something beautiful and unexpected happened. They cancelled the game. Imagine that. Finally someone had the guts and the decency to stand back and say, "Today is not the day for cheering. It is a day to mourn." And maybe the umpire would have wanted the game to go on . . . perhaps. But the game can always go on at a later date. In addition, families of athletes and celebrity friends should not be put in the awkward position of having to say, "Oh, it's okay. I'm sure my husband . . . my father . . . Umpire Bob would have wanted you to play on."

When a tragedy occurs, especially at a high-profile event, people need to be given a chance to stand back and take stock of their lives. They need to go home, sit with their loved ones, and reflect on the wonderful gift of life. They need to explain to the children in attendance about what happened and how precious the gift of life truly is. And that applies to the guy selling peanuts, the fan in seat section 9, as well as the celebrity throwing out the first pitch.

That's why, when the bowling continued in lanes three and five, framing the dead body on lane four, I was thrown aback for a few seconds—that is until I started laughing hysterically.

The aging man bowled a strike, turned and high-fived the other players on his team, and then dropped DRT, as one of my former residents would say: Dead Right There. It was a heart attack, a stroke, or arrhythmia—something killed him. He was obese and in his late fifties, clad in a blue gaudy bowling shirt and khakis. We arrived at the bowling alley in Pittsburgh in a specially outfitted emergency physician vehicle. Typically, our runs were cardiac or respiratory arrests, fire or motor vehicle accidents as well as entrapments, shootings, baby deliveries, and so on. Joanne, the other physician, and I grabbed our equipment and rushed inside to the sound of balls hitting pins with that unmistakable resonant ceramic clashing. He was dead on lane four. No one was really doing much of anything when we got there.

We immediately began CPR, shocked him a few times, and gave him heart-starting drugs, but this guy's heart had no electrical activity at all—straight as an arrow. It was a typical pre-hospital cardiac arrest; I've been on so many now I can't count or remember them all. What struck me, though, about this death was that the bowlers on the adjacent lanes continued rolling. Here we were, hovering over a dead man on lane four, and the bowling teams from Joe's Bar and Bill's Auto Painting couldn't have cared less. In fact, someone actually pushed some of our equipment out of the way so as it would not interfere with their game. One man rolled a strike in lane five. He yelled out, and there were a few pats on the back followed by a fist-pumping gesture, only a few feet away from where I was trying to put a tube in the man's lungs. I placed the tube and looked over at my colleague who was checking for breath sounds.

"How would you like dying on a bowling lane while everyone just kept bowling beside your dead body?" I asked Joanne, with a great degree of disgust in my voice.

Without missing a beat, she glanced up at me and answered with a grin, "Depends on how much I liked bowling." And with that simple response, she burst my bubble of indignation and in addition caused me to bruise my lower lip biting it to keep from laughing so hard. As we covered the blue-faced man in his blue shirt with a white hospital sheet, I could've sworn I saw him smile.

Chapter Twenty-seven

www.helpme

At first I thought she might be faking it, as she sat slumped over in the wheelchair. She was young, thin, and pretty, as her husband hurriedly pushed her into the ER. I meandered into the room with minimal urgency, swallowing the last bit of my low-fat turkey sandwich from Starbucks mixed with a gulp of decaf coffee. I gave them a quick, "Hi, I'm Dr. Profeta," and then kicked down the lever holding the bed rail up and reached across to help the young woman onto the gurney. She flopped heavy in my arms, like a wet bag of newspapers; this was a slap upside the head, telling me her condition was very serious. While I talked to her husband, I quickly did a primary survey: assessed her airway, looked at her pupils, yelled for a stat head CT scan, sank an IV line, and checked her blood sugar. The saliva was thick in my throat; something catastrophic was happening to this young mother of two small boys, and after some 50,000 patients I knew pretty early that I was not going to be able to fix it. As we rushed the young woman off to get a CAT scan, I went back and forth with her husband.

"She's had a severe headache for two days, vomiting . . ."

"Does she use any drugs, or have health problems . . . diabetes?"

"No, she's completely healthy; doc, is she going to be all right?" he asked.

"Don't know yet. Has she complained of fever, double visions, night sweats?"

"I . . . I . . . don't know. Is she going to live?"

"Is she on any medications?"

"Should I call her parents?"

I knew what the CT scan would show before the first digital image fully materialized. A digital hourglass hung on the computer screen; the sand was running out. Her brain was bleeding, and this was going to end with her death.

Now I could stop this story here, and you would be left with another tragic tale, the sad death of a young woman with much life yet to live. Instead, I am going to tell you a heroic tale of how this woman's plight was thrust into to blogosphere and into the conscience of nearly 200 physicians around the country. And how they scrambled to this woman's rescue, walked side-by-side in cyberspace-consultation and how they cried with me and her husband when she died.

To set this story, I have to go back a few years to an innovative young physician who had had enough of the plodding routine of a surgical residency program at a prestigious Boston hospital, a clinical arm of Harvard University. I suppose he had one of those 'AHA moments' where he said, "What the hell am I doing here?"

And while most weary young physicians have that same AHA moment, often several times each day, few have dropped out of a prestigious surgical residency to start a blog site. His website was to be for physicians only, a place where they could escape, discuss politics, blast lawyers and insurers, lament about Medicare, and share clinical pearls—essentially talk about all those things in the cyber equivalent of the high school chess club. Over time, though, it has become a social escape for tens of thousands of physicians wanting to 'get things off their chests'. It was in cyberspace that this young woman's fate hung, her last days, hovering between the touch of her family and an electronic bulletin board blasting her condition along the wireless modems of these thousands of physicians, all hell-bent on trying to save her life.

It was early in the morning, and she was my first case of the day. Her condition was grave to the point that I needed to put her on life support. Just prior to this drastic step, her husband leaned over and gave her a gentle kiss on the lips knowing deep down it would probably be their last. Once the tube to breathe for her was placed into her lungs, she stabilized but still remained in critical condition. I spoke with the neurosurgeon, and we both felt she would be best served by being transported to our larger hospital. I arranged for an ambulance and a critical-care transport team, and sat down in my office, flipping though medical books, seeing if perhaps I was missing something. Nothing came to mind.

Then it hit me! Post her case on the doctor's blog, in real time, and see if any other physicians might have an idea, or have treated anything similar. Who knows, we both might get lucky.

In order to draw as much attention as possible to this urgent plea, I opted for the attention grabbing title: **I Just Had a Horrible Case.** I laid out the situation as quickly and as accurately as I could: Thirty-Five years old, healthy, no significant past medical history, with multiple sites of brain hemorrhage on head CT, etc, etc. There must have been a sense of urgency and despair in the way I posted the case, because the blog exploded with suggestions from neurologists, internists, infectious disease experts, ER docs, and other specialties—all making suggestions, offering guidance, and a shoulder to lean on, a comforting cyber-hug, that said: "You are not alone, we are here with you." So in this small ER north of the city, in the early hours of the morning when children were starting their day and coffee was being dished out in central standard time cafes, physicians from across the country were poring over books, racking their brains, digging into their case files, and trying to save a young woman whom they only knew as: "The Horrible Case".

About 48 hours later, after screen upon screen of comments offering insights into cerebral vasculitis, steroid management, antiviral therapy, immunosuppression, the thread was punctuated by the following . . . Pt died at 0900 . . . husband age 35 . . . 2 children.

And while this may sound like another natural end to the

story, it doesn't stop here. A few months later, the blog had a contest for the best emergency medicine post. Well, a physician in Texas nominated my post, and around late November I was the proud, anonymous recipient of a Sermo (the blog site) choice award for the outstanding post in emergency medicine, which came with a $500 honorarium that accompanied the award. And there it sat in my home office, along with my check for $500.

And as sure as I sit here, I gloated over that check for a solid two weeks, fingering the print, smelling the paper, and snapping it against my palm . . . 500 smackers. I had made up my mind. I was going to cash it that week. You see, anyone can 'justify' a wrong decision, if you think about it long enough. But as seems to be the case with me more recently, when I am faced with these moral conundrums, God tends to step in and help me resolve the issue, usually in his favor.

We have some twenty physicians that rotate through various days and shifts at this small community ER we staff. When you take into account that fact that we see some 20,000 people each year, the chances of me working at any particular hour are only about one in twenty. Now calculate the chances of someone coming to the ER at the exact moment in time where I am thinking about how best to spend their $500—it must border on infinitesimal. But of course, that is exactly what happened.

"Hey Profeta, get in here, someone wants to say hello," shouted the voice of my colleague Dr. Smith. He came out of this room where he was sewing the lip of some kid that crashed sledding.

And there he was: her husband and one of her children. "Dr. Profeta. . . remember me. . . you took care of my wife." He held out his hand. I clutched it in both of mine.

"Of course, I remember. How are you and your children doing?" I asked, motioning to the one with a big piece of gauze sticking out of his mouth.

"We're doing okay," he said, but his eyes gave away the truth.

I tried to flash him a smile, shuffling my feet and looking at the floor. At that moment I had a suspicion that God was laughing at my expense, like watching your child do something stupid but harmless. The check was a goner. "I'm driving the kids to Florida next week; we've never been on vacation before."

I nodded my head and shuffled my feet some more. "Uhhhh . . . I meant to call you. I have a check for $500 sitting on my desk for you." A look of confused surprise crossed his face. "You remember how I posted your wife's case in real time on this doctor's blog? Well, this other doctor nominated it for an award on this blog and it won. So stop by tomorrow and I'll give you the check."

The next day he stopped into the ER with his children in tow. I give him the check, and he just looked at me in bewilderment.

"I don't know what to say. I just . . ."

I interrupted him and cleared my throat. "Listen . . . just go have a good time, and get something cool for Christmas, you all deserve it."

And with that he left.

In all 200 doctors reached out through cyberspace and offered support for this dying woman. Nearly 200 doctors held my invisible hand, and cradled my invisible head. These doctors cried, cheered, laughed, and reflected on the sacred bond for which they were entrusted. Nearly 200 doctors bore witness to the mystical nature, the godly energy that binds us like cement to each other. And at $2.50 a pop, I'd say I got a good deal.

Chapter Twenty-eight

"I Treat Everyone the Same"

"The check is in the mail", "I promise it's just between you and me," and "I treat everyone the same." These are three of the biggest falsehoods that come to mind, outside of the few that I can't really put in print. The third pretense is the biggest lie in medicine. It is one of those nails-on-the-chalkboard proclamations, the verbal equivalent of chewing on a metal fork. And it is most often a pathetic attempt by the nurse or physician to explain either their inability or their lack of desire to relate to people from a variety of social, ethnic, and religious classes by indignantly sticking their chest out and bellowing, "I treat everyone the same!"

My response to this self-indulgent verbal pat-on-the-back is simple: Considering that everyone is different, and that our ER population is a remarkably balanced cross-section of American society, from Hispanic to African-American, white Anglo-Saxon Protestant to Jewish, from Muslim to Catholic, filthy rich to poor white trash, it is a safe bet that nurses and doctors treat most people in a manner that does not make them comfortable and in many instances they do not appreciate.

There is a famous ancient story about Rabbi Hillel that, when challenged to teach the entire Torah (the five books of Moses) while standing on one foot, he responded, "What is hateful to you, do not do unto others; the rest is an explanation of that. Now go study." This is an obvious predecessor of the Golden Rule, most commonly recited by our Christian brethren. But herein lay the confusion. What is hateful to one may be comforting to another. What is comforting to some may be hurtful to another. I have learned that the only way to know is by getting to know your neighbor or the people you treat.

There have been numerous studies examining how different racial and ethnic groups perceive the attitude of medical staff in regards to their care, pain control, and the administration of healthcare services. In addition, there seems to be a range of patient expectations when it comes to discussing healthcare problems. Studies show that certain ethnic classes want and expect significantly more content when confronted with medical test results, whereas others want a more concise and to-the-point description. Some cultural groups greatly enhance the perception of pain, whereas other groups feel the request for pain relief to be a sign of weakness. One patient can find your explanation to be over their head, while the same explanation to another may be welcomed for being on their level. In many ways the ER is the Ellis Island of our time: the place where all of society congregates, waiting for a chance to pass into the promised land of medical salvation, a cacophony of accents: from Russian, Chinese, Spanish to urban slang and rural drawl.

Getting back to the Golden Rule, I think the implication is that God wants you to make your neighbor comfortable, to know your neighbor. How could you possibly do unto others if you have no idea how those others will respond? Over the years I have noticed rural Caucasian males, especially laborers and craftsmen of European descent, tend to be very stoical when it comes to pain medications. I have seen these jean-clad tough guys come in for kidney stones, amputated digits, and open fractures requesting nothing more than ice packs. Their high blood pressure, fast heart rates, and beads of sweat on their forehead and upper lip give away their agony from the pain they feel. I offer them morphine or something of similar strength, and they casually shoo me away, "Naw, Doc, I'm okay . . . maybe later." That's when I do unto them.

"You know, if it was me on that table, I'd be crying like a baby. I had a kidney stone once and it felt like I was trying to crap out a whole beef roast with the bone in it. Now listen, let me give you some morphine to take the edge off and keep the pain from getting worse. There is no need to act tough here . . . you don't want to be in pain, and I don't want you to either." I don't wait for a reply. I just quickly turn to the nurse and ask her to bring some pain medication. And you know what? They never turn down the request.

The easy way out would be to just tell the patient, "Let me know when you want something." But that would be a failure on my part to get to know the patient, to do unto others, to speak their language, and to understand their fears.

So often, nurses and medical students will be irritated by a patient who comes into the ER with a simple complaint in the middle of the night: the poison ivy at 2:00 A.M., the sore throat at 3:00 A.M., or the mild cough at 3:45 A.M. Oftentimes the nurses will roll their eyes and toss the chart with a resounding thud into the to-be-seen rack, and walk off mumbling about the absurdity of this complaint at this hour of the morning. By getting to know this population of patients—the so-called denizens of the night—and really exploring their motives, here is what I have found: Many of them are really there seeking help for drug or alcohol addiction, depression, or other emotional problems. They just don't want to talk about it with anyone other than the doctor, so they make up a false complaint. Most of all, they don't want to run the risk of seeing someone they know in the ER waiting room. Others are homeless and just want a place to hole up for a few hours, get a cup of coffee, some crackers, or perhaps a bed. Many of these patients just can't sleep or get rest from their condition. They figure there is no problem just coming into the ER. There is nothing more miserable than trying to sleep with a severe sore throat or congestion. Some of these patients work night shifts, just like us, and have maybe an hour break to come into the ER. Others are single parents of limited means and small children. They sneak out of the house while the kids are asleep; this is the only time available to get medical care for them. Finally a few of them are just at the end of their rope and want their problem fixed regardless of the time. But, then again, the only way to know that is by getting to know them.

So in the ER I try to do unto others. I try to make them all comfortable. I try to do what is best for them as an individual. I try to put my prejudices and judgments aside, but most of all: I try to treat each patient uniquely and get to know them, if just for a bit. And like most physicians and other healthcare providers, when I leave the hospital I tend to forget all of these niceties and focus on my own self-comfort and pleasure. You see, once I leave my house of god, the ER, and go home to my family and my close friends

. . . well, I tend to treat everyone the same.

Chapter Twenty-nine

"You Don't Understand . . . I am Going to Die"

I think she was about 35, slightly heavy, and had dirty-blonde hair. Her face was marked and ruddy with years of tobacco and alcohol abuse, and perhaps just a tired, strained life. She came into the ER sitting bolt upright on the gurney, grasping the side rails, and complaining that she could not breathe. She undulated and rocked back and forth on the cot in a sick symphony, calling for anyone who would listen. Her yells were palpable and disturbing to the patients on the other side of the curtain who were within an earshot.

"Help me, I can't breathe, I can't breathe," she cried, over and over again. Sweat beaded on her brow, her body strained. But her oxygen level was perfect, her chest was clear, and her EKG was normal.

"Calm down," I told her, "you're going to be all right. Slow your breathing and tell me how long you've felt sick." She shook her head as if shooing me away, not wanting to talk about it, not wanting to explain.

"I can't breathe," she repeated over and over again. I did all I could do to get some useful information, but the locked-in fear on her face told me she was lost in another world, or perhaps another time. Nothing seemed to be helping; oxygen did nothing to alleviate her distress. Her chest X-ray was normal.

"Did you take something, a drug . . . anything?" I pleaded.

Again she shook her head in disgust. "I can't breathe," she said, but softer now.

"Calm down," I reassured her. "We're going to take care of you; you're moving air well, and the oxygen level in your blood is good."

Suddenly, she sat bolt upright, digging her nails deep into my arm, pulling my eyes into hers. "You don't understand . . . I AM GOING TO DIE!" And with that exclamation, she fell back hard, let out a final sigh, and her heart simply stopped. I was dumbfounded.

One of my colleagues, Tom, peered around the corner, hearing the commotion as did everyone in the vicinity. We immediately started CPR, placed a breathing tube in her, and injected every imaginable medication in an attempt to save this woman. But in the end her heartbeat just ran out. We were left with the sobs of other patients and their families who bore witness to this sad event.

"What do you think happened?" Tom asked.

"A massive blood clot in her lung, tore her aorta, or blew a hole out of her heart wall; take your pick."

In retrospect, I knew we would not have been able to save her in any of the above scenarios. But I still felt profoundly sad and was left with a sense of helplessness. Why had this person been allowed to come into my life for these fifteen tragic minutes? What did I really contribute to her final restless hours but a sense of my own profound frustration? She knew something in the very depths of her being: she knew that she was about to die. It was as if this were her final salvo, a way to tell the world that she was here, and that she would be remembered, if only by a stranger.

And what of God, what was his role in this? Her time was his time, and we were simply spectators in this event. Or was it more of a lesson in mortality, our fragile existence, or that dying is always loss, and that we should grieve even for those we know only for a brief moment, or as a pleading voice on the other side of the curtain?

Chapter Thirty

"Stop Him"

I don't remember his name. He was a big guy: forty years old or so, maybe five-eleven, and weighed at least 250 pounds. That night it was catastrophically busy. We had patients in every bed in the ER, and they were overflowing into radiology and in other parts of the hospital. We were most likely in the midst of a flu season.

As time passes, most patients just blur into a chief complaint: they aren't Mrs. Jones with chest pain or Mr. Brown with a stroke. They become the acute MI or the CVA, as if their identity is forever tied to their illness. I do know that this gentleman has no idea of the name by which I summon him from my memory. To me he is simply . . . the voice.

"I'm having trouble breathing, coughing a lot, that kind of stuff. I work at Ball State and went to a Med-check earlier today, and they said I had bronchitis and put me on this stuff." He handed me an asthma inhaler, some prednisone, and I think an antibiotic.

That's just great, I thought to myself, exasperated: This guy comes in only twelve hours after a checkup and is surprised he hasn't gotten any better. He hasn't even given the medications a chance to take effect. And now, to top it off, I have to waste my time convincing him that the earlier diagnosis was correct, and then he'll be angry that I'm not going to do anything else and that he wasted all his time tonight.

Mind you, in my self-serving egocentric style, I have already pegged this guy. I have formulated all this without even laying a hand on the patient. Damn, I'm good. So I did a quick evaluation; he sounded a little wheezy perhaps, or maybe I imagined it to feel better about the time spent. I gave him a breathing treatment and then ran out to attend to a patient who was most certainly in greater need. An hour or two more went by, and I'd forgotten about my nervous doughboy who would not let his meds kick in. A nurse reminded me that he was still in the examination room and asked what we were going to do with him.

"Tell him I'm tied up and I can't get back there. Sign him out and reassure him it's just bad bronchitis, and he'll be fine in about three days. Oh, and give him a work release. That's probably what he is here for anyway."

I tended to some paperwork as the gentleman passed by in front of me onto the way out of the heavy metal security doors of the ER.

"Thank you," he told me with a conciliatory closed-lip smile as he approached the heavy exit doors. His demeanor and walk seemed to be affected by the nurse's comforting explanation; the doors snapped open with a loud clang. That's when I heard it inside my head . . .

"Stop him."

"Sir . . . STOP, stop, hold on a minute." I quickly moved over to where he was standing with his wife. I stood for a second and just sort of stared, not sure as to what to say. In my head I clearly thought I heard a voice telling me to stop him, a voice as clear as if someone stood next to me and shouted into my ear; this was not to be ignored. And in the same instant, I knew deep down what is was. In all honesty I was a bit freaked out and asked a slew of questions: Who was it? Was that me? Or was it something I imagined or overheard? It was just a simple "Stop him." No bolts of lightning struck the ER; he had no yellow halo of celestial color around him; I didn't see an image of baby Jesus or the Buddha in a water stain on the floor; it was simply a voice, but it was as real to me as the keys I now type out this account on.

I stammered a bit, falling completely out of the superior doctor's role. I felt like a juvenile in the principal's office (a feeling

I once knew all too well). "Sir, can I ask you to do me a favor? I have been very busy tonight, and I did not give you the attention that I think you deserve. I know you have been here a long time, but if you go back to your room and let me start all over, I'll waive the bill." He had no reservation whatsoever and was easily escorted back to his room.

The nurse peered at me as if I were crazy. "You're going to start all over with this guy, a new chart, vitals, everything?"

"Everything," I said. "Something doesn't make sense . . . just trust me." She shrugged her shoulders, gave me one of those looks, and nodded.

One hour later I had this man in the intensive care unit on high-dose heparin with a diagnosis of a massive pulmonary embolus: a condition that would most likely have killed him shortly after leaving the ER.

I went home and reflected on how close I came to contributing to this man's death, to playing a part in making his wife a widow, and leaving his children fatherless. And I thank God for giving me the ears to hear and the 'common sense' to accept the improbable.

I still on occasion hear that voice but it is much softer now, sort of a gentle prodding that says, "Slow down, you're in a hurry. You're not listening to your patient. It's your patient who is asking for help, not you." Who is speaking? Well, I think it is God. You may think it's my subconscious mind. Maybe they're one and the same. Either way, perhaps we all have to listen a little more. I just wish I could completely convince myself of it. In the mean time, I'll keep working on using my ears more and closing my mouth. I've noticed it's quieter, anyway.

Chapter Thirty-one

The Rich Get the Worst Medical Care

Control is hard to give up, no matter what you do for a living. But, if you are in charge of a lot of people, are used to getting your own way, and you are someone who causes people to jump whenever you snap your fingers, it's even harder. In an uncertain world, one thing is for certain: the medical care you receive will suffer because of it. I bet I have done more than 2,000 rectal exams in the past 15 years. Considering the fact that my index finger is only four inches long, I have performed a digital exam on more than 220 yards of rectum throughout my career (a very long par three, to be exact). One thing I have noticed is that I can't tell a rich asshole from a poor one. That is, until they open the other end of their digestive tract, and start talking.

"Sir, how long have you had chest pain?" Sweat poured from the fifty-something, graying man with manicured nails, Italian loafers, and a smoking-hot secretary.

"Just call Dr. Doolittle. He's my heart doctor [gasp] . . . just call him."

"Sir, he's not a cardiologist. He's a surgeon. Now, listen. How long have you had pain?" I implored him further, the EKG showing diffuse ST elevation, indicating an impending heart attack.

"Get my cell phone . . . Annie," he said, rolling his sallow eyes toward his secretary. "Just call him . . . Dr. Doolittle . . . he's a friend of mine. We're golfing buddies; he'll know what to do." He writhed around in the bed, clutching his chest even more, refusing the IV until his friend was called, and requesting a Vicodin for the pain.

"Do you have a heart history, high blood pressure, diabetes?"

"Call Dr. Welby, he's also a friend of mine . . . tell him Jack's in the ER. He'll know who to call; I play golf with him, too."

With a rising sense of urgency, I further explained, "He's an orthopedist, sir. Listen to me. We need to get a line in you and . . ."

"Listen, just call one of them; Dr. Welby, Dr. Doolittle, or Spock . . . I know him, too. He's a good friend."

"Sir, he's a pediatrician."

"I don't care!" he snapped at me, his voice rising above the din of the emergency room. "JUST DO IT!"

Everyone fell silent as a long pause hung over the room. That was when I looked him straight in the eye, leaning close so as not to lose his attention. I locked him into my gaze and spoke just above a whisper, "If you don't stop . . . shut up for five seconds . . . and let me take control and do my job . . . you are going to die. Do YOU understand what I am saying?"

He looked at me in astonishment, a mask of terror now gently turned into one of relief spreading across his face. He nodded silently in acquiescence, finally surrendering. Minutes later, the pace in the ER was at full speed. Lines were placed; nitroglycerine, heparin, aspirin, and oxygen were administered. He was expedited to the emergency angioplasty where the cardiologists, whom he did not know and hadn't golfed with, were able to open the vessel and save his life.

He sent me one heck of a gourmet gift basket a week later.

Far too often the rich get the worst medical care. For the most part, they have no idea that this is the case. With wealth comes easy access, and anything easy is hardly ever worthwhile. Easy access is an assured recipe for drug addiction and inappropriate diagnostic testing. I am saddened at how many people with authority and people of wealth fall victim to prescription drug abuse, unnecessary medical tests, inappropriate operations, and unwarranted diagnostic workups.

I am certain it exceeds the general population, but how

exactly do you do a study? They get a doctor into their confidence (they golf, dine, or travel together), and a casual phone call becomes a request for a sleeping aid, a pain pill, and since they are friends, the request is of course seamless in its simplicity. One phone call results in a bottle of Ativan, another call results in an MRI, and a third nets epidural steroids and a bottle of Vicodin with three refills. In time, the requests pile up and the hapless doctor is caught up in a web of addiction, diagnosis, and medical procedures that take on a life of their own.

The doctor enjoys the perks of having such an influential friend, while at the same time aware that he is being all too cavalier in the practice of medicine. In time it all catches up to them when that patient finds their way to the ER suffering from withdrawal, an overdose, or some complication relating to an unnecessary operation or diagnostic test. By that time this patient of privilege has fostered relationships with a number of physicians, calling them all by their first name and inviting them to their suite at the arena or the party that everyone wants to attend. They will cultivate, nurture, water, and grow an entire garden of physicians: the internist, the orthopedist, the ENT doc, and the ER standby. Neither the doctor nor the patient means for this to happen; it just happens. At one end the patient is in search of control over that which they have little control, i.e., their years on earth; while at the other end, the doctor is in need of a sense of importance, confirmation that they are one of the best in their field. After all, they are so and so's doctor. This happens because these patients are also simply better able to take charge of the situation than the physician. It is the nature of the beast; it is why they are so successful, and it is the precise reason why they have more unnecessary testing done, more operations, more second, third, and fourth opinions, and ultimately higher narcotic addiction potential.

So, when the patient is finally admitted with an overdose, a suicide attempt, or in a withdrawal state, I'll typically call around to the local pharmacies and make a list of all the prescriptions filled and who wrote them. Usually, there are five to seven doctors in the web; each one of them is overprescribing narcotics on an individual basis, let alone as a group. I'll call each one of them privately and tell them that I think their patient is addicted to narcotics, and that I have asked Social Services to see about their addiction and about getting the patient some help. Here is what is amazing: None of the physicians are ever surprised.

"I suspected as such."

"Yeah, I was concerned about the same thing."

"I thought so."

"You know, you are probably right . . . a good thing they came in."

While all suspect a problem, rarely do they approach the patient with that prospect. They want someone else to do their dirty work, to take control of the situation, to alleviate them of the burden. And when it finally happens, they are usually relieved to be rid of this 'friend'.

Fear of losing control or the need for maintaining control: It's what drives so much of our decision-making, but once relinquished it is also a profound relief. I believe that is one of the reasons people have a hard time finding God. It is because at some level they have to give up control and say, "I'm in your hands." Me, I'm horrible with it, and I admit it. I am one of those fly-by-the-seat-of-my-pants spiritualists who tend to only invoke God when things are going badly, or when I truly need someone else to take control. Sitting back and keeping my mouth shut at my kids' baseball games, and not playing the role of coach, was as hard for me as a root canal without anesthetic. So, I am no role model for this exercise, but give me a few more years.

Of late I have made a profound attempt to invoke God's name a little more, even if it means just asking for help in placing an IV, calming a patient, or dealing with the quirks in my interpersonal relationships. In a sense, I am giving up a degree of control and asking for help, playing second fiddle to a higher power. I have found it unbelievably refreshing, though I still feel like a hypocrite, since I don't do it all the time. My sense is that God doesn't even care: for Louis, it's a start.

Chapter Thirty-two

Crop Dusting with Prozac

Why not? We add fluoride to our drinking water, ten essential vitamins and minerals to our kids' cereal, and iodine to our table salt. Why not crop dust with Prozac, or at least add it into all of Starbuck's mocha java lattes? Toss a sprinkle into the 7-11 cherry slurpy-machine slush, and the filtered end of Marlboro Lights: I figure that would cover a solid 75 percent of the population.

I'm not making fun of depression; on the contrary, I think that it has reached epidemic proportions and has become the great masquerader of medicine. Ask any ER physician who is the most difficult patient to care for: it's not the combative alcoholic, the infant with meningitis, or even the gunshot victim. It's not the car accident survivor with multiple fractures, or the drug-overdosed patient. It's the forty-year-old woman with a history of migraines, fibromyalgia, chronic fatigue syndrome, irritable bowel syndrome, mitral valve prolapse, and a whole host of drug-related allergies.

As much as you try not to be prejudicial, you know what is in store for you. You muster all of your empathy, you put on your best compassionate face, you practice your "I seeeee's" and your "Oh myyyyy's," but you know this will be a no-win situation before you ever even meet the patient. The history will be extensive with complaints pertaining to nearly every imaginable organ system: chest pain, headaches, muscle pain, abdominal pain, ringing in the ears, blurred vision, palpitations, nausea, poor appetite, fatigue, irregular periods, and on and on. The symptoms will be completely nonspecific, spanning the spectrum of illness from malaria to cancer, from heart disease to pregnancy. The blood tests, CT scans, X-rays, and EKGs will yield nothing. The patient will once again become frustrated at your perceived lack of medical insight and will launch a verbal salvo of how they have seen Doctors 'A through M', and they have not been able to figure out what is wrong. That is when you casually mention stress or depression being a potential factor. Then, all hell breaks loose.

"Ma'am, I've got good news! All of your tests look great. You're not having a heart attack, no anemia, your white blood cell and thyroid tests look great; there's no sign of anything serious going on."

"Well, there has to be something. I don't understand how I can feel so rotten; I've been to Doctor 'A,' Doctor 'B', and last week I saw Dr. 'R', and Dr. 'P' sent me back to Dr. 'A', but 'A' says the problem is clearly something Dr. 'B', or perhaps Dr. 'K', should take care of."

"I see . . . oh my, I can imagine how frustrating that must be for you. What does your family doctor say about all this?"

"He doesn't know anything; I stopped going to him because he thinks it's all in my head, and I know it is not all in my head."

"I see . . . hmmmm . . . well, let me ask you something; you have all these tests, nothing ever shows up, no matter what doctor, so where do you go from here?"

"What do you mean?"

"I mean, you've already spent years chasing a diagnosis that has never materialized, and in all likelihood I doubt you'll ever really get one. And, let's face it: you're not dead, and nothing has fallen off of you. Sure, someone will eventually tell you that you have fibromyalgia or chronic fatigue syndrome, or perhaps even some odd form of multiple sclerosis, but you'll never really get any better. I think it is possible that your family doctor was correct, that this could be a physical manifestation of major depression."

Now in ER heaven, her response would be:

"You know, doctor . . . you may be right. What do we do next, is there a medicine for depression I can start, or can you recommend a therapist or psychiatrist? What do I need to do to get better?"

But, most of the time, this exchange happens in ER hell:

"I am not depressed. I don't know where you went to school or who you think you are, but you don't know me. I am sick; this is a real problem. Get out of here. I am not going to listen to you anymore. I want your name; I'm complaining to your boss about you!"

And that is why these patients go on year after year without ever getting better, being funneled from one doctor to another, and shuffled from specialist to specialist, and from clinic to clinic. In time they will collect diagnoses like some collect Hummel figurines, shopping for a doctor to give them that one diagnosis that they can hang their hat on, that one illness that will explain all of their maladies to them and allow them to avoid the real issue: that they are major depressed.

As sexist as I sound (and I don't mean to be), this symptom complex is typically feminine. Why? I don't know, but I have my theories. Men seem much more amenable and even relieved to learn that depression or anxiety is causing their symptoms. We ignore pretty much every ache and pain until the last possible moment. This is probably due to the fact that the specter of illness hovering over the guy's head is coronary artery disease, a heart attack, and a quick death. We don't want to know. It's what's in our psyche: here one minute gone the next. We tend to walk through life at times feeling like we're in a sniper's sight. As a man, I know that we're idiots when it comes to our health. We always think we're going to die. Every cold is a death sentence, every episode of vomiting a tumor, but we'll wait until tomorrow to get it checked out. We are the walking dead; thus there is a level of profound relief in knowing it is 'just stress', or 'just anxiety', or 'only a panic attack'. We also don't mind losing as much. Guys are very forgiving of each others' 'perceived' character weaknesses, and we don't view anxiety or depression as such.

Women, on the other hand, are more attentive to those lumps, bumps, aches, and pains. They can recite the statistics and health risks that threaten their own bodies. And besides, they have to hurry up and schedule their chemotherapy, because Jimmy has travel soccer next week and Suzy has a dance class. You see, the specter of breast and ovarian cancer justifiably weighs very heavy on their psyche. From a preventive medical standpoint, this is good. But the constant bombardment in the media of the high risks of these cancers—along with the rise in female coronary artery disease, obesity, spouse abuse, and the illness de jour ads in every woman's magazine—has scared women to death. Check out any supermarket tabloid rack and you'll understand. It is not enough to be a mother, a wife, a career woman, and to raise a family; they need to have a malady to truly make them a success, to be a survivor, a modern woman of the 21st century.

I think deep down inside, that most of these women know intuitively that their problem is not life threatening. They seem to have a much better awareness of self, better insight into the workings of their own body. It's like taking a test in school; when you miss an easy answer and it costs you the 'A', you don't feel stupid, you feel angry. I think women get angry because they feel like they should have seen it coming, or can't come to grips with why they feel depressed, especially when they 'have it all'. To a woman, being told they are depressed is like telling them that they are a failure.

While as men we're just damn glad that we're not having a heart attack and can wolf down another piece of cheesecake. Besides, by the time prostate cancer typically becomes an issue, we've forgotten what we used it for anyway.

This leads me to the question, "Why is there so much resistance to depression for being the underlying cause of all their symptoms?" I place the blame for this resistance squarely on the shoulders of one person: media mogul Ted Turner.

As I have said throughout this book, there seems to be a God-given need to be connected to the world, to feel that you are part of something bigger than yourself. But with the advent of 24-hour cable news networks and their scrolling teletype with NEWS ALERT in bold letters, that connection has increasingly become a world full of suicide bombers, missing children, tsunamis, tribal wars, and amber alerts. It is reminiscent of the Don Henley song, *Dirty Laundry*:

We got the bubble-headed bleach-blonde who comes on at five,

She can tell you 'bout the plane crash with a gleam in her eye.

It's interesting when people die...

Give us dirty laundry.

Unfortunately, someone forgot to tell Ted Turner and his like that, on occasion, the laundry needs to be washed. We have become mentally soiled with the stream of bad news that permeates the airwaves, the constant political bickering of the left and the right, the endless hours of economic woes, impending disasters, 'food Nazis', and boundless statistics portending our doom, that the sins and the weight of the world make those of us looking to connect with others physically sick.

So when a person comes to the ER with symptoms that, in most probability, are a somatic form of depression, it could be that at some level I am confirming their biggest fear: that life sucks, that the world is a big septic tank of despair. Their anger may be that one last attempt to deny their own self-imposed reality. Show me a person who fills their body with booze, cigarettes, drugs, and junk food; and in time, I'll show you a broken shell of a body, regardless of that person's mind. Show me a mind that is filled with reality TV, 24-hour news with its countless images of death, world despair, famine, poverty, and war; and in time, I'll show you the broken shell of a spirit, regardless of that person's body.

So, how do we solve this epidemic of depression? Is crop dusting with Prozac really the answer? How do we stop the illness before it progresses to doctor shopping and a litany of non-diagnosis? How do we encourage people to turn the damn TV off, close the paper, and just for a while live in the moment? In classic Judaism, it is expected that on the Sabbath, one does not watch TV, work, turn on the lights, and so on. I like to think that God had the 21st century in mind when he said: now is a time to rest, to refresh your soul, to take stock of what is important. Now is the time for love, for prayer, and for family. After all you are human, and in time if you truly want to feel really connected, you will on occasion need to wash the laundry.

Chapter Thirty-three

"The Best Doctor in the World"

A few years back, a well-known thoracic surgeon, "one of the best in the world," they say, came to our emergency room with his young son, who had the unfortunate experience of getting a fishhook stuck in his leg. He insisted the patient be seen only by him; after all, he was "one of the best in the world," they say. He hurriedly directed the nurses to retrieve a plastic surgical tray, a scalpel, forceps, a good light source, wound cleanser, sterile gloves, lidocaine, and a host of drapes and ancillary equipment he would need to perform this delicate, subcutaneous, barbed foreign-body extraction. He orchestrated the department and the techs with maestro-like precision, everyone doing their part with speed and synchronicity that can only be described as magical. While he was busy flittering around the department, directing the woodwinds and prompting the snares, I snuck into the room. With a quick fisherman's trick, I snapped the hook out of the young man's leg. Not a whimper was heard.

The surgeon scrubbed, gloved, and gowned, and with grand flare, entered into his patient's room. I, on the other hand, on that less-than-busy morning, went back to my task of doing the crossword, pausing to contemplate number four across: a six-letter word for peace. Shortly thereafter the surgeon exited with a perplexed stare above the surgeon's mask.

"How did you get that out?" he confusingly inquired of me.

"I'm not telling you," I replied without even looking up. A palpable pause hung in the air.

"No, really, no joking, how did you do it?" he implored with more urgency.

"Listen," I said, looking him straight in the eyes. "Five

minutes ago, you thought there was absolutely no way that anyone other than you could possibly know more, or perhaps have greater insight as to how to treat this patient. And now, after the fact, you want the benefit of my knowledge, my help, and my expertise? You want to tap into my years of training and intellectual sacrifice that ended up with me being here at this point of time saving your child from certain peril? I don't think so." I smiled sarcastically.

He laughed a bit and acquiesced to my good-natured ribbing, yet remained anxious for the opportunity to learn two lessons, one being the string technique of fishhook removal. I have not teased him about it since. After all, he might have to bail me out some day.

It has gotten to the point that no one can just go to a doctor anymore. That person has to be the best. After all, who in their right mind would go to any physician unless they are absolutely the best? So, with that, our community has the world's best oncologist, cardiologist, general surgeons, urologist, pediatrician, and on and on and on. In fact, I think our hospital alone has at least fifty of the best doctors the world has ever seen. You would think with all the 'he's-the-best, she's-the-best praise', Indianapolis would see more ill pilgrims than the Fountains at Lourdes. However, that is not the case. Why? Because just one state over you will find the absolute best oncologist, cardiologist, general surgeon, urologist, internist, and pediatrician in the world.

I did my medical school training at Indiana University and my residency at the University of Pittsburgh. While in medical school, I was in awe of the knowledge and diagnostic skill most of my clinical teaching physicians held. We were young, naive medical minds whom were easily impressed. The talk among the students was that 'Dr. A' was world renowned. 'Dr. B' was one of the most famous in his field. Everyone in America knew 'Dr. C', he had published the most medical literature. You have to get a letter of recommendation from 'Dr. D', because everyone knows he is clearly the best in the world. To us, it was as true to fact as the number of bones in the human body. But surprisingly, after moving to Pittsburgh for my residency years, a mere five-and-half-hour drive to the east, no one knew Doctors 'A, B, C, or D'. And if they did, it was because they had trained together, or perhaps read some study co-authored by that doctor. Oh sure, occasionally, some bit of notoriety did make 'A, B, C, or D' stand out. Perhaps they found the most appropriate treatment for a certain kind of cancer, authored an important chapter in a national medical textbook, or served on the governing board of their respective college of medicine. But at no time was the adjective phrase of 'the best in the world' used to describe them. That moniker was saved for about fifty physicians at the University of Pittsburgh.

If you gathered a Jew, a Catholic, a Buddhist, and a Muslim together in one room and asked them to pick the best religion in the world, you'll get four different individual answers. Ask them to pick the worst and you'll get hundreds of answers. Just as it is futile to try to establish the best faith, it is pure folly to label any physician as the best, though it does not prevent us from trying. Hospitals pay a fortune gathering patient satisfaction data, manipulating statistics, and posting billboards and advertisement proclaiming:

"Number one in cardiac care"

"The most trusted name in medicine"

"Doesn't your child deserve the best?"

"Midwest GI number one, when you can't go number two"

These same hospitals and watchdog groups pay very close attention to statistics detailing surgical infection and complication rates (morbidity), death rates (mortality), patient complaints, and malpractice, trying to manipulate the data to show that they are the best. But did you know that some of the highest morbidity and mortality rates clearly come from some of the 'world's best surgeons and most prestigious medical centers'? How could that be, you might ask? It's because they tend to take care of the sickest patients and the ones most likely to suffer from complications. For example, take the thoracic surgeon who only does redo-coronary artery bypass grafting. He or she operates primarily on patients who have had prior bypass surgery, and usually a host of other illnesses. Naturally this leads to higher complication rates, higher incidents of post-operative fatality. How do you evaluate the success rate of an infectious disease specialist who practices in a community that is impover-ished and without mass transit or adequate Social Service assis-tance? Certainly patient medication noncompliance and poor follow-up care lead to a higher death rate for that physician's patients. Or how about an ER physician who works at half the speed of his colleagues, sees a fraction of the number of patients, and hand selects the easiest cases from the to-be-seen-rack? Surely statistics would come to support that that person is 'the best'.

I have had the opportunity to moonlight (work part time) in rural ERs throughout Pennsylvania and Indiana. For the last 14 years I have practiced in a large, big-city, teaching hospital. I am disturbed when a physician from a big city or major tertiary referral medical center rolls his or her eyes and comments about some patient coming in from 'Podunkville', or 'St. Elsewhere', offensive tag lines used to describe any facility (especially rural or poor healthcare facility) that are not their own. They usually make some crass remark about how the doctors there "Don't know shit." They puff out their chest and sigh in disgust at the imposition of having to accept a patient who needs the services of a more specialized facility. That physician will then operate or treat the referred patient. He will bill for his or her services, and usually get paid. The physician will then dictate a consult letter to the referring 'don't know shit' physician, which will have key lines which read, "Thank you for entrusting me with the care of your patient," or "Thank you for your kind referral of this gentleman or interesting case." Unfortunately, that physician will do all of this while bad-mouthing the same physician or medical center to his subordinates. It is a verbal salvo aimed to demonstrate that "I am the best in the world." In reality, most of these tertiary medical centers and their corresponding practices would not be able to function financially if it were not for the referral base of the rural hospital system. What is more disturbing is the filtering down to the residents and medical students, creating a Third Reich mentality of academic superiority and the false poisoned notion that 'Dr. Mad Dog' is somehow the best. In actuality, he merely represents the worst that medicine has to offer.

The reality of the situation is that you can bet that for every patient transferred to the 'ivory tower' institution, there are twenty others that some 'Podunk doctor' has cared for, cured, rehabilitated, and operated on without the help of the academic center. In addition, I can tell you without any hesitation that very few of these Gestapo physicians would be able to walk in, operate, and keep pace with the rural surgeon who practices without the benefit of three OR nurses, float techs, surgical backup, resident labor, and a host of consult services that a large hospital provides. In addition, many of these physicians are so specialized and so focused that they have in all actuality lost the ability or desire to care for the common malady, the fishhook in the thigh. Fortunately, those self-congratulatory physicians are the exception and not the norm, but they do create an educational tumor that needs excision.

By now you are probably convinced that the rural, small-town physician is the best. I spoke with Dr. Doug Smith, one of our urgent care physicians who used to be in family practice in a small rural community. He jokes about how patients in small towns are no different from our population. They will look you in the eye with absolute conviction and tell you that every doctor in their community is a quack...except their physician, of course.

Their doctor is the "best in the world."

It is evident to me that everyone knows 'the best doctor in the world'. It's their doctor. So, if everyone's doctor is the best doctor in the world, how does one truly find the 'best-best doctor in the world?' Is it by virtue of the most publications, the highest cure rate, the lowest mortality rate, or the fewest number of malpractice cases? Is it by virtue of peer review, financial ability to advertise, largest marketing budget, or nicest cookie platter delivered on the holidays? I don't know the answer to that, but I'll let you in on a little secret: If you want to know who the best-best surgeon is, ask the OR nurses and the anesthesiologists. They'll tell you. Inquire about who gets the most bent out of shape, throws equipment, curses, and yells at the nursing staff , medical students, and residents when the going gets tough? That's the one you want to avoid. The others are the best in the world. Who is the 'best-best physician'? Ask the ER doctor. They'll tell you who answers their pages in a timely fashion, readily listens to what the ER physician has to say, and easily makes follow-up appointments available for their patients in the ER. Which physician comes in expeditiously without argument when it is suggested they do so? Those are the best doctors in the world. That kind of attention translates to care for the patient in the hospital, the office, and the community.

I have come to realize one thing: Choosing the 'best-best doctor' is like choosing the best religion; it is thirty percent timing, thirty percent trust, thirty percent faith, and ten percent luck. Add an extra hundred percent if they take your HMO.

My children recently asked me, "Daddy, how many ER doctors are there in your group?"

"Something like 25," I answered.

"Who's the best?" my youngest asked.

Naturally, I said, "Me, if you catch me on the right day."

"What do you mean?" my twelve-year-old questioned.

"I mean, if I'm swimming in Lake Monroe and a snapping

turtle floats up and latches onto my balls, whoever is in the ER at that time… well, they're the best doctor in the world."

Chapter Thirty-four

Can You See God Through a Video Lens?

A while back I was camping with some friends in the Quetico Provincial Park in Southern Ontario. For anyone who has any taste for the outdoors, this is one of those places that you have to go in your lifetime. It is a series of lakes, rivers, streams, and tributaries that course through the Canadian territory and inter-mingle with thousands of lakes in the Northern Minnesota Boundary Waters. You can drink fresh from the streams; eagles catch the air currents over pine-covered forests. Moose and deer wade through the shallows, and black bears survey the landscape. In the morning a fine mist hangs over the waters like the scent of a loving wife, hugging the surface in a gentle embrace. It is a world of loons, frolicking beavers, wild blueberries, and has some of the finest walleye and smallmouth bass fishing in either country. The rocky landscapes are dotted with vistas like Indian paintings, where each view and secret cove is more spectacular than the next. And if it were not for the hordes of biting black flies, I would say it is the closest place on earth to Eden. It is a sacred land with only the soft splashes of canoe oars, a sanctuary devoid of any motorboats. It was on one such trip that I saw God, and the best part about it is that I had five witnesses.

We had been canoeing and fishing all day; it was comfortably cool, the dusk was settling, and we had finished tying up the canoes, cleaning the plates from our dinner of fresh fish and wild rice. We had chosen a campsite at the end of a small lake, fed at one end by a good-sized river and emptied at another by way of a very large waterfall. The current leading into the falls was quite strong and dangerous, and we would never consider navigating our canoes in the vicinity of the fleeing water. We were perched on the cliffs overlooking the falls below us and the lake in front of us. The roar of the falls was amazingly peaceful, and the mist carried up by the force of thousands of tons of water pounding on the rocks created a gentle humidity that covered us like a blanket of cool summer wine. As the day closed, we sat upon the rocks, sipped Scotch whisky, and smoked a few cigars. I suspect each of us was, for a brief time, reflecting upon how beautiful the scenery was, how perfect the day had been, and how at that pinnacle moment of our union with nature that it could not get any better. We were wrong.

Movement in the woods next to the falls caught our eye; just below us we could make out a large animal, moving beneath the trees, a deer or a moose perhaps. That's when a huge timber wolf climbed out of the forest and stood on a large rock, jutting into the lake framed against the mist of the waterfall. We sat there stunned, not wanting to move, not wanting to say a thing. It sniffed the air, cocked its ears a bit, and then bobbed and tossed its head back, flattening its ears and gazed at the sky. She was a wild debutante displaying her finest, as if to say, "I know you're watching." It gently toed the water, then cautiously waded in and swam across the river a mere twenty yards in front of a waterfall that could have certainly swept this gorgeous creature to its death. But it swam across on a straight line, undeterred by the flowing current, barely even being nudged off its course. Reaching the opposite side, its paws struck the sandy bottom, and the wolf slowly climbed out lifting her legs in a gentle dance to dry land. Her silver coat shook and diamonds of water flew into the air splashing gems against the rocks. And without so much as goodbye, she faded into the pines, silver, to brown, to dark.

For a moment none of us spoke, we just looked at each other. The first phrase muttered was, "Oh my God." I had tears welling up in my eyes and I was not alone. This was my version of

Michelangelo: my Pieta . . . my David. As I sit here typing, I can still smell the waterfall; I can hear its rumble and feel it beating in my chest. Each movement of the wolf is ingrained in my mind; I know it like I know each freckle on my child's nose. I close my eyes, and I sit here years later, and it is still as beautiful, still as amazing as ever. And I still find myself thanking God for that moment.

"I wish I had my camera out," said Mike.

"Why?" I asked, incredulously.

"You know, so we could have a record, showed it to some friends."

"Then you wouldn't have gotten to see it."

"Sure I would, just through the lens."

"Then you would not have gotten to SEEEEEE it," I emphasized.

My point is that seeing something like this magnificent wolf cannot be captured in a two-dimensional digital reconstruction. You have to see it with your own eyes; it has to speak to your senses: the touch of ground under foot, the mist, the cold air, the sounds of a pounding waterfall, everything has to be in harmony for you to SEEEEE it. You cannot fully experience your daughter's first recital if you are peering at her through a video lens; you cannot feel the tinkle of the keys, the missed notes, or see the gentle rustle of her new dress against the piano bench. You can't really see your sons first hit, feel the dust rising from the diamond, hear the gentle whoomph of him leaping onto first base, if your eye is pressed against the camera's eyepiece. You can't see your child's first play, notice the subtle smiles and waves, the rocking uncertainty of memorizing speech if you are working on the focus or the zoom. You can't see; you're not really there.

But for a whole new generation of parents, the world is passing them by; their child's greatest moments are lost, or the chance to squeeze the hand of your spouse, to exchange smiles, glances and moments of pure joy, because we are too busy taping what we should be experiencing. We are missing God's presence, we are missing angels dancing, and we are missing heaven on earth, all for the sake of a few gigabytes of video file on our I-Mac.

We are taping the present so that in the future we can watch the past that we never saw when it was happening. We have turned into thousands of water buffalo, jostling for positions at the front of our watering hole: a darkened auditorium, hoping to capture on video that one special moment in time, when we instead should be capturing them on the hard drives of our souls. You can't see God through a video lens. In time my mind will fade, my eyes will falter, but as I go gently into that good night, I will have with me my most prized possessions . . . my memories.

Epilogue

I exited Room Nine, the soft light slowly retreated back into the sanctuary from where it came. With a gentle clack, the brushed steel knob engaged the door frame. The hallway seemed brighter and more inviting. I glanced down at my watch: 3:30 A.M.

The nurse caught up to me in the corridor. "So, did God have anything to say?" she asked half-jokingly.

I paused, looked back at the door, shook my head, and gave her the faintest of grins. "Not yet, but then again we're just getting started."

A puzzled look danced across her mask of fatigue. "Maybe, you weren't listening well enough," she replied.

"Maybe," I answered, my smile widening; I turned to walk down the hall.

"So?" she called out after me. I stopped and looked back over my shoulder.

"So, let's call social services and see about getting him a room somewhere in psych." Balancing the clipboard in my open palm, I motioned to the door. "But first let's get him a cup of coffee, perhaps a meal tray, or better yet one of those donuts, and let's listen to him for a while. I bet he has some stories to tell."

BOOKS

O is a symbol of the world, of oneness and unity. In different cultures it also means the "eye," symbolizing knowledge and insight. We aim to publish books that are accessible, constructive and that challenge accepted opinion, both that of academia and the "moral majority."

Our books are available in all good English language bookstores worldwide. If you don't see the book on the shelves ask the bookstore to order it for you, quoting the ISBN number and title. Alternatively you can order online (all major online retail sites carry our titles) or contact the distributor in the relevant country, listed on the copyright page.

See our website www.o-books.net for a full list of over 500 titles, growing by 100 a year.

And tune in to myspiritradio.com for our book review radio show, hosted by June-Elleni Laine, where you can listen to the authors discussing their books.

mySpiritRadio